VOLUME 4

BILINGUAL EDUCATION: CURRENT PERSPECTIVES

Education

CENTER FOR APPLIED LINGUISTICS

Library of Congress Catalog No.: 77-80381
ISBN: 87281-066-6

November 1977

1611 North Kent Street
Arlington, Virginia 22209

Printed in the U.S.A.

Preface

The Center for Applied Linguistics, which serves as a national center for policy, research, and information in language and linguistics in the United States, is pleased to make this survey of *Bilingual Education: Current Perspectives* available to decision-makers and others interested in this important and rapidly-developing field. These volumes, and the conferences from which they came, reflect a concern on the part of the Center that significant decisions are constantly being made regarding bilingual education--by judges, lawyers, legislators, policy planners, administrators, teachers, parents--frequently in the absence of adequate information on which to intelligently base those decisions.

Believing that informed decisions are crucial in efforts to effectively meet the needs of non- and limited-English-speaking students, the Center brought together leading specialists in the United States concerned with bilingual education from a number of disciplines, to provide the most complete compilation of information possible on this subject. The results reflect the complexity of the situation, as well as the relative paucity of research data resulting from an almost total lack of federal funding for research. It is a national scandal that the United States has spent over half a billion dollars on bilingual programs, and less than one-tenth of one percent of this amount on the basic research needed to improve the quality of programs. If defense systems and medical drugs were developed in the same way, we would certainly fear for our national safety and health. But in education, programs continue to be planned, and legislation implemented, with little thought for research. It is ironic that although Canada has probably spent one-tenth as much money on bilingual programs as the United States, most of the research available on bilingual education has and continues to come from Canada. This is a situation which policy-makers urgently need to remedy, if efforts to insure equal education opportunity for limited-English-speaking students are to proceed with any confidence.

The Center for Applied Linguistics has been active since its inception in 1959 in the fields of teaching English to non-English speakers and the teaching of foreign languages, and in recent years has given priority to work in bilingual education in an effort to improve the quality and effectiveness of this approach to language instruction. Currently, the Center, in effect, serves as a national resource center in the field of bilingual education. Through its work in this field and its other research and service projects dealing with language and education, the Center has developed considerable capabilities for assisting schools and communities to meet the needs of multilingual populations.

The Center is grateful to the Carnegie Corporation of New York for providing financial support to this project, and to the Office of the Commonwealth of Puerto Rico in Washington, D.C. for their encouragement and funding of the development of a grant proposal.

I want to thank Leann Parker, who served as coordinator for the series of conferences, and helped see these publications through the press. She did an excellent job of a very complex task, and deserves our gratitude.

Rudolph C. Troike, Director
June 1977

Foreword

The nature of language and its relationship to culture is such that it is unfeasible to attempt to change one and not the other. Attempts have been made to teach English as a second language, as in the case of Puerto Rico, allowing the Puerto Rican society to maintain its native Spanish language and culture. In the case of Puerto Rico, the learning of English has become a necessity brought about by its close political and economic ties to the United States. In the past, the emphasis in the school system was placed on the study of English in order to Americanize the island.

Traditionally, the teaching of English as a second language in the United States has been geared toward the complete acculturation of foreign and ethnic groups to the mainstream of American society, without allowing these ethnic groups to use their mother tongue for any other purpose than social communication in their communities. However, the Puerto Ricans have determined that it is their right to keep Spanish as their first language and learn English as a second. In Puerto Rico, Spanish as the native tongue has been maintained for use not only in social settings but in overall economic and political communications, with English used as the language of technology.

The knowledge of more than one language has become a necessity in the world we live in today. Our close ties to each and every other member of the world has also made it necessary to understand the different cultures which comprise our society, without imposing any one language or culture on any member of that society.

This concern about the nature of language and culture and related education policies, both in the United States and Puerto Rico, led the Office of the Commonwealth of Puerto Rico (OCPRW) to inquire more about what is actually happening in the field of bilingual education in terms of research and practices. As the Center for Applied Linguistics shared many of these same concerns, the OCPRW decided to support a proposal by CAL to develop an in-depth, objective state of the art study of the field. We hope that the papers presented in these volumes will bring a greater understanding of the issues and the state of our knowledge about various aspects of bilingual education and will provide a basis for sound decision-making in the future.

Office of the Commonwealth of Puerto Rico in Washington, D.C.

June 1977

Introduction

One of the most noteworthy and controversial movements in American education over the past decade has been bilingual education. The concept of providing instruction in their own language to students who come to school speaking little or no English was given federal sanction in the 1968 Bilingual Education Act (Title VII, Elementary and Secondary Education Act). Since that time, bilingual education programs serving numerous language groups have multiplied across the country as federal, state and local funds have been allocated to this purpose. Momentum was increased by the landmark *Lau v. Nichols* decision in January 1974. The Supreme Court found that providing identical education programs for both English- and non-English-speaking students did not constitute equal education opportunity and that special language instruction was necessary to allow non-English speakers real access to the content of the education services. Although not strictly mandated by the *Lau* decision, bilingual education has been seen by the Office of Civil Rights (DHEW) and subsequent court rulings as a major way of meeting the special needs of these students.

As public monies have been spent, and as linguistic and cultural minorities have vied for visibility and power, questions about bilingual education have abounded. The questioning of fundamental claims has recently been accentuated with the advent of Congressional hearings in preparation for rewriting the federal legislation in 1978.

It is in this context of controversy that the Center for Applied Linguistics, long a supporter of greater education opportunity for American minority groups, felt the need to take a hard and objective look at what is known about the undeniably complex nature of bilingual education. Many academic disciplines are researching relevant aspects of bilingualism, language acquisition and teaching in a bilingual situation from their own perspectives. People in other fields such as law, legislation and education administration are more involved in policy aspects of bilingual education. Each group deals with the issues in its own way and each has much to contribute in terms of understanding the complex issues; yet, each needs access to sound information on which to base further research and analysis of the field and for decision-making.

Recognizing the need for an objective, multidisciplinary and comprehensive look at the field of bilingual education, CAL sought support for a project which could produce such a state of the art survey. Sharing the Center's concern, the Office of the Commonwealth of Puerto Rico in Washington (OCPRW), under the directorship of Jose Cabranes, provided support for the development of a grant proposal which was subsequently funded by the Carnegie Corporation of New York. The OCPRW has continued to assist the project through the participation and advice of Carmen Delgado Votaw.

CAL commissioned state of the art papers on four general areas of bilingual education: social science research, language and linguistic research, legal precedents and aspects and education perspectives and education research. Each paper formed the central focus for a separate conference at which it was discussed and elaborated on by specialists from different fields within that discipline. The conferences were attended by invited representatives of various federal agencies and other organizations, whose questions and comments brought useful direction to the discussions. During the spring of 1977, a final panel representing the several fields was convened. Participants at this session included authors of the major state of the art papers and specialists from a variety of fields. Their task was three-fold: To share information across disciplines; to synthesize what each could empirically say about various issues and questions in bilingual education; and to assist in the development of a guide to pertinent research findings for decision-makers.

This series of volumes presents the collection of major review papers and viewpoints of the discussants. Each of the first four volumes presents the particular perspective and research of a particular area. Following the meetings, the writers of the major papers were permitted the opportunity to revise their papers. Discussants' papers, although written in reaction to early drafts of the major papers, have been included for their insightful comments and frequently detailed reviews of the literature of specific areas of the various fields. The final or "synthesis" volume of this series has been designed to summarize and organize the findings in the various fields, and to direct the reader to relevant discussions in the papers presented in the other volumes.

CAL expresses its gratitude to the participants at each conference for their enthusiasm and contributions to increasing the understanding of bilingual education (see the acknowledgments for a list of conference participants). In particular, we thank the authors of the major review papers: Joshua A. Fishman, G. Richard Tucker, Herbert Teitelbaum and Richard Hiller, and George Blanco.

The project was also assisted by the able guidance of a steering committee and several advisors whom we would like to thank for their participation in this effort. Special thanks go to

Rudolph C. Troike and Roger W. Shuy, whose overview of the issues as well as their support and recommendations provided valuable direction throughout the project. Appreciation is also due to Shirley Brice Heath, whose insight and suggestions during the development of the synthesis volume were particularly helpful.

The Center also wishes to express its sincere appreciation to the Carnegie Corporation of New York for its generous and indulgent support of the project, and to project monitors Vivien Stewart and Frederick Mosher for their advice and assistance throughout the project.

Without the assistance and moral support of a number of competent persons working as a team it would not have been possible to plan and carry out the multitude of details and preparations essential to making the conferences run smoothly and to readying the papers for publication. Thanks also go to CAL's Bilingual Education and Indian Education Programs for their assistance throughout the project. We particularly thank the following staff for their participation in the synthesis meeting: Rosario C. Gingrás, Tracy C. Gray, Gilbert García, Lance Potter, and Phyllis Nudelman. We express our special appreciation to Cynthia H. Gusky for her expert secretarial assistance, to Diane Bartosh for her care in the copyediting of the papers and in their final preparation for publication, and to Sonia Kundert for typing the first final manuscript.

L. Leann Parker, Project Coordinator
June 1977

Contents

Keynote

The Education Perspective

George Blanco

*America is God's Crucible, the Great Melting Pot where all the races of Europe are melting and re-forming! Here you stand, good folk, think I, when I see them at Ellis Island, here you stand in your fifty groups, with your fifty languages and histories, and your fifty blood hatreds and rivalries. But you won't be long like that, brothers, for these are the fires of God you've come to--these are the fires of God--Germans, Frenchmen, Irishmen and Englishmen, Jews and Russians--into the Crucible with you all! God is making the American....*So proclaims Israel Zangwill in his play, *The Melting Pot* (1909). The striving for oneness and equality has been a powerful, motivating factor in the founding and evolution of the United States. *E pluribus unum* is a motto recited by many generations of schoolchildren in testimony of the belief that this country derives its strength and character from its multinational roots. These roots, as in a living plant, support and provide nourishment for the exposed branches, leaves and flowers; yet the roots themselves remain hidden. The "one out of many" motto has conveyed the idea that immigrants are expected to conform to one lifestyle and to one language if they are to succeed and reap the full benefits offered by this country.

In 1972, Congress passed the Ethnic Heritage Studies Act (P.L. 92-318), which challenged this time-honored concept of sameness by recognizing "...the heterogeneous composition of the Nation and the fact that in a multiethnic society a greater understanding of the contributions of one's heritage and those of one's fellow citizens can contribute to a more harmonious, patriotic and committed populace...." What caused this apparent about-face in the thinking of America? Would this type of philosophy not undermine the very tenets on which the country had been founded? Were we not all expected to be Americans with the same language and culture? This change in attitude was a slow evolutionary process that came to maturity during the 1960's when many traditional values were being questioned, and the idea of what it meant to be an American was being examined.

Out of this decade of turbulence came a concern for the individual and for identity. Such concern, making itself felt on various fronts--social, economic, political, educational, linguistic--forced the nation to re-examine its attitudes. Suddenly America was no longer the "crucible." The same country that had always believed in its ability to assimilate the masses into one society where everyone was equal, now seemed bent on destroying that great philosophy of oneness. The Black-White dichotomy, anti-war demonstrations and race riots of the decade fed the fires of discord. The anger and hostility of these groups went much deeper than the evident discrimination.

The concept of a multicultural nation may have begun with the Black-White problem, but it soon encompassed non-Black ethnic identities, dimensions and subcultures. The 1960's saw the emergence of the youth movement and culture, the women's movement, the sexual revolution, the Gay movement--all demanding equal rights. This seeking of the recognition of individuals as human beings--whether it was on the basis of race, sex, ethnicity or language--had a definite influence on American education.

Multicultural education programs have been the result of America's recognition of its pluralistic society. Through multicultural education, Native Americans, European Americans, Afro-Americans, Mexican Americans, Asian Americans and other ethnic groups may participate in curricular programs designed to meet their special needs. "The school should help our nation become an 'open society' in which a variety of cultures, value systems, and life styles not only coexist, but are nurtured...Individual and group differences would be prized, not merely accepted or grudgingly tolerated, and every person would have equal access to what they want from and can give to society (Della-Dora and House, 1974)." It has been this salutary climate for cultural diversity that has made the initiation and expansion of bilingual programs possible.

The awareness of our being a pluralistic society, however, also had its roots in the appalling failure of the education system to meet the needs of linguistically and culturally different groups. For example, the Report of the NEA-Tucson Survey on the Teaching of Spanish to the Spanish-Speaking (NEA, 1966) had a far-reaching influence on subsequent legislation for children of limited English speaking ability (LESA). This report brought to the public eye the tremendous disparity between the educational achievement of Mexican Americans and the general student population. According to a 1960 California study, more than half of the Spanish-surnamed males and nearly half of the Spanish-surnamed females 14 years of age and over had not gone beyond the eighth grade. In contrast, only 27.9 percent of the males and 25 percent of the females over the age of 14 in the total population had not gone beyond the eighth grade. The study also revealed that over 72 percent of the males in the total population and 75 percent of the females had gone through at least one or more years of high school. By contrast, only 48.5 percent of the Spanish-surnamed males and 52 percent of the females had achieved this educational level. Of the total population, 23.4 percent of the males and 19.4 percent of the females had completed one or more years of college. Yet only 8.8 percent of the Spanish-surnamed males and 6.2 percent of the females had reached this level of education. The study also reported that the Spanish-surnamed population of the Southwest did not fare as well economically as the general population in 1960.

The cycle of poverty, plus the low esteem in which minority groups were held, contributed directly to such distressing statistics. These social, economic and educational conditions added support to the subsequent legislation and education reforms to meet the needs of LESA children. The gradual acceptance of the United States as a multicultural country, however, provided the necessary climate in which to begin the revolutionary bilingual education movement.

NATURE OF BILINGUAL-BICULTURAL EDUCATION PROGRAMS

Goals of Bilingual Education

There is much evidence in the literature to show that the goals of bilingual education are compatible with the goals of general education. While one can argue about the role of education, educational philosophers (Dewey, 1966) believe that the school must not only meet the needs of the individual, but that education must be based on the intensive activities and needs of the person to be educated. Thorndike and Gates (1966) indicate that the "ultimate aim of education for man is to secure the fullest satisfaction of human wants." Along these same lines, the National Council for the Social Studies, in its preliminary position statement, *Ethnic Studies Curriculum Guidelines* (forthcoming), proposes a change within our educational system to respect, rather than reduce, ethnic diversity in America. The Council insists that this proposed change is in keeping with such national ideals as freedom, equality, justice and human dignity. Addressing the concept of diversity, Castañeda, Herold and Ramírez (1975) propose a new philosophy of education which they call cultural democracy. Cultural democracy "stresses the right of every American child to remain identified with his own home and community socialization experiences." They go on to say that bilingual education embodies this philosophy by emphasizing the maintenance of the child's first language for instructional purposes while learning a second language. If the education system purports to uphold our national ideals and to transmit the culture of our society, it is duty-bound to provide equality and human dignity to its students by recognizing their linguistic and cultural strengths, whether they happen to be Anglo, Mexican American, Puerto Rican American, Black or Asian American.

A commonly accepted definition of bilingual education in this country is the one set forth by the U.S. Office of Education (1971):

> [Bilingual education is]...the use of two languages, one of which is English, as mediums of instruction for the same pupil population in a well-organized program which encompasses all or part of the curriculum and includes the study of the history and culture associated with the mother tongue. A complete program develops and maintains the children's self-esteem and a legitimate pride in both cultures.

Although English is a necessary component of bilingual education, the teaching of English as a second language (ESL) alone does not constitute a bilingual program. ESL means the field of teaching English to speakers of other languages (Alatis, 1976). Teachers of English to Speakers of Other Languages (TESOL) identifies three education approaches utilized to teach U.S. students of limited English speaking ability (TESOL, 1976): (a) bilingual instruction including an English as a second language component; (b) monolingual instruction including an English as a second language component; and (c) monolingual instruction without an English as a second language component. Of the three approaches, TESOL recommends the first as the preferred model. The second model may be necessary in some cases, but "under no circumstances does the third, monolingual instruction without an English as a second language component, provide equal educational opportunities to students of limited English proficiency, and it is categorically rejected as an alternative instructional model for their education." The third model was used almost exclusively prior to the passage of the Bilingual Education Act in 1968.

The consensus of writers in the field of bilingual education reveals that the primary thrust of bilingual education lies within the cognitive and affective domains, rather than the linguistic realm. The main purpose of bilingual education is not to teach language per se, but to provide students with the opportunity to acquire knowledge and skills through the language they know best while at the same time adding English to their linguistic repertoire. While it is obvious that the linguistic dimension is basic and necessary to the concept of bilingual education, it is felt that the primary goal of bilingual education is to allow children of limited English speaking ability to participate successfully in the education process (Andersson and Boyer, 1970; Saville and Troike, 1971; von Maltitz, 1975). Such authorities address the importance of language in bilingual education and they are convinced, along with others (UNESCO, 1955), that the use of native language (as opposed to another language) is not only the best language for instructional purposes, but that its use in school can only enhance the child's self-image and esteem for his own culture. Thus, as a result of participating in a bilingual education program, the child should acquire competence in two languages. These writers are firm supporters of maintenance, rather than transitional, bilingual education programs to develop fully biliterate individuals capable not only of understanding and speaking, but of reading and writing two languages on a wide variety of topics.

The cultural goals of bilingual education call for a recognition of the child's home culture and its inclusion as part of the instructional program. Language and culture are inextricably interwoven and language is the most identifiable and basic exponent of a culture. Besides language, the bilingual program often incorporates other cultural elements of the children's home, be it music, cuisine or folklore. One of the most inclusive statements concerning the role of culture in the bilingual program (or, in their words, "multicultural program") is that made by Castañeda, Herold and Ramírez (1975):

> A truly comprehensive multicultural program would include these curricular objectives (language, holidays, historical figures, and traditions), but would be addressed as well to those features of a child's socialization experiences which have shaped his preferred or dominant learning style. In other words, the basis for a child's learning about his own and other cultures must encompass the language, heritage, values, thinking and motivational frameworks with which the child is initially familiar...His language, heritage, values, and modes of cognition and motivation can subsequently serve as a basis for exploring and developing selective loyalties to alternative expressions of thought, values, and life styles.

> There, the child would learn to function completely and effectively in, as well as to contribute to development of more than one cultural world.

This statement underscores the necessity of including elements of the child's home culture in the curriculum. Nelson Brooks (1972) outlines 25 elements of "deep" culture with emphasis on the personal; topics range from language to religion and duties. Although there is an increasing number of programs and curriculum materials which include these elements as an integral part of bilingual education, the truth of the matter is that not enough is known about specific cultures to have a serious impact on teacher training and on school programs.

The cognitive, linguistic and cultural goals of bilingual education are interrelated and are, in turn, closely linked to the affective goals. The importance of self-image may, in the final analysis, be the single most important outcome of bilingual education (von Maltitz, 1975):

> The concepts and practices involved in bilingual-bicultural education projects have as a major goal leading students to believe in themselves, in their basic worth as human beings, and in their native capacities. One important factor in reinforcing these pupils' self-confidence is having the language they speak acknowledged and respected; another is having as teachers, and models whom they can emulate, persons who use that language and stem from the same cultural community as their pupils.

Speaking to the issue of the education of Mexican American children, Cárdenas and Cárdenas (1972) propose a theory of incompatibilities which prevents minority children from successfully participating in the education process. The writers indicate that an instructional program developed for White, Anglo Saxon, English speaking middle class students is not adequate for non-White, non-Anglo Saxon, non-English speaking, or non-middle class students. More specifically, they feel that there are five major incompatibilities (Cárdenas and Cárdenas, 1972)[italics mine]:

1. *Poverty*. The absence of success models in the family, inadequate housing, malnutrition are some factors that promote the development of differing concepts toward education and that influence the development of poor children.

2. *Culture*. The school has traditionally known little

about the minority students' home culture and its traditions, values, and orientation. The result has been one that has created negative stereotypes and culturally irrelevant instructional materials.

3. *Language*. When the Spanish speaking child is placed in an English language school program, he cannot participate successfully since there is an incompatibility of language. ESL programs have been inadequate by themselves because the Spanish speaking child is deprived of cognitive and skills development until he learns to communicate in English. Further, excluding the home language creates in the child a sense of inferiority.

4. *Mobility*. Families in lower income brackets are very mobile in their attempt to find employment. Children in such families often find themselves attending two, three or more different schools in the same year. The mobility is incompatible with school programs based on continuity and sequence.

5. *Societal Perceptions*. Minority children tend to perceive themselves in a negative way. The typical instructional program is designed for children with positive self-concepts and armed with certain prerequisite knowledge and skills. Minority children often do not fit in the mold and they tend to develop a negative self-concept.

The authors feel the areas of culture and language are of utmost importance in the curriculum, not solely from the point of view of cognition and the performance of pupils, but from the perspective of how the child will feel about himself. This notion of improving the students' self-image is considered so vital that one can conclude from the foregoing that it is one of the major objectives of bilingual education today. This writer, however, questions the effectiveness of such an effort in a transitional bilingual education model which does not give equal stature to both the home language and English.

MODELS OF BILINGUAL EDUCATION PROGRAMS

Program Design

A number of writers have proposed many models of bilingual education programs according to such factors as the treatment of the language, time allotments, school subjects, pupil characteristics, goals and staffing patterns. In 1963, Stern defined bilingual schools "one-way" or "two-way." "One-way" were those programs in which one group of students learned through their mother tongue and through a second language--the majority-group language. "Two-way" was the term used to designate programs in which two linguistically different groups of students learned through their respective mother tongues and through the other's language. These groups were broken down further according to whether the languages received equal time and treatment. Other characteristics of this particular model include such factors as whether the mother tongue or the second language is added and whether students are mixed or separated by language. The time and treatment given to each language are also considered.

Mackey (1972) proposes a scheme whereby bilingual education programs may be classified into any of eight basic types of curriculum models which could theoretically yield 90 patterns accounting for the structure of the home, school, area and nation. He is not suggesting that such a large number of bilingual education programs actually exist; rather, he is categorizing every possible type of variable which would yield a different program of bilingual education. Mackey suggests the following basic types of curriculum patterns (1972) [italics mine]:

1. *Type SAT (single-medium accultural transfer)*. In this model the school may transfer the language of learning from that of the home to that of the school. It could be completely accultural by taking no account of the language of the home.

2. *Type SAM (single-medium accultural maintenance)*. The home language or dominant home language is taught as a subject without being used as a medium for other subjects of the curriculum.

3. *Type SIT (single-medium irredental transfer)*. The home language or dominant home language is used as a medium of instruction.

4. *Type SIM (single-medium irredental maintenance)*. The dominant or formerly dominant language is maintained as a school subject.

5. *Type DAT (dual-medium accultural transfer)*. For political or prestige reasons, this type prepares pupils to receive the rest of their education in a language which is not dominant in the home, usually a language of wider communication.

6. *Type DIT (dual-medium irredental transfer)*. In areas long dominated by a foreign language, the medium of instruction may revert to the language of the home and the foreign language is kept as a subject.

7. *Type DDM (dual-medium differential maintenance)*. This

type maintains two languages for different purposes and the difference may be established by subject matter.

8. *Type DEM (dual-medium equal maintenance)*. For political reasons, both languages are given equal treatment. This may be done by alternating days, weeks, months, or even years from one language to the other.

In contrast to Mackey, Saville and Troike (1971) propose three basic types classified by language treatment. The first type recommends instruction in the basic subjects in the child's first language while learning English as a second language. The amount of English is increased in grades K-two, and becomes the language of instruction for certain subjects once the child has gained adequate control. In grades three through eight, equal treatment is given both to the first language and English. The second type begins like the first: In grades three through eight, English becomes the language of instruction for the majority of courses and the first language is maintained in some subject areas. For communities wishing rapid acculturation, a third type is presented which is similar to the first type for grades K-two. The first language, however, is phased out altogether in grades three through eight.

Fishman and Lovas (1970) classify bilingual programs into four categories:

Type I — Transitional Bilingualism: The native language is used only until the children adjust to school and are able to participate in academic subjects in the second language.

Type II — Monoliterate Bilingualism: Programs of this nature have as a goal the development of oral language in the native language and the second language, but reading is taught only in the second language. Programs of this type of orientation represent an intermediate step between language shift and language maintenance.

Type III — Partial Bilingualism: These programs have as an objective fluency and literacy in both languages, but literacy in the national language is limited to some content areas, preferably those that have direct relation to the culture of the linguistic group.

Type IV — Full Bilingualism: In programs where full bilingualism is the main goal, students are taught all skills in both languages in all domains.

While these and other writers (Paulston, 1975; Spolsky et al, 1974; Valencia, 1969) continue to suggest "ideal" types of bilingual education programs designed to meet the needs of specific populations, it appears that programs are usually restricted by state and federal legislative guidelines. The overwhelming compensatory nature of U.S. bilingual programs has already been mentioned. Within these limitations, though, a variety of programs has surfaced. González (1975) reports five major types of bilingual education programs today:

Type A Programs:	ESL/Bilingual (Transitional). Strictly remedial/compensatory orientation.
Type B Programs:	Bilingual Maintenance. Student's fluency in another language is seen as an asset to be maintained and developed.
Type C Programs:	Bilingual/Bicultural (Maintenance). Similar to Type B, but it also integrates "history and culture" of the target group as an integral part of curricular content and methodology.
Type D Programs:	Bilingual/Bicultural (Restorationist). A strong attempt is made to restore to children the option of learning the language and culture of their ancestors which may have been lost in the process of assimilation.
Type E Programs:	Culturally Pluralistic. Students are not limited to a particular target group. Rather, all students are involved in linguistically and culturally pluralistic schooling.

The U.S. Commission for Civil Rights (1975) reports visitations by its staff to four different language group bilingual education programs: Philadelphia, PA (Puerto Rican), Johnstown, CO (Mexican American), Rock Point, AZ (Native American) and San Francisco, CA (Asian American). At Johnstown and at San Francisco there were bi- and monolingual classrooms at each grade level, so that children from both language groups could select their preference. The Rock Point and Philadelphia schools include all the children enrolled in the school.

Program Scheduling

The models presented previously serve as bases for practitioners in the field for the implementation of programs. Bilingual education has already been defined in this paper as the use of two languages for all or part of the instructional program. But what, exactly, is taught in a bilingual education program? Is it primarily a language program? Is the same material taught first in one language and then repeated in the other language? To begin to answer these and other questions, the Board of Education of the City of Chicago (1974) presented a list of seven statements indicating what bilingual education is and seven statements declaring what it is not. In part, the document proposes the following: "It [bilingual education] involves the entire curriculum being taught in two languages....It is not exclusively a language-teaching program which excludes math, science, and other curriculum areas." In line with those statements, the U.S. Commission for Civil Rights (1975) succinctly states the general content of bilingual education programs:

> The content of what students learn in a bilingual bicultural classroom is similar to what students learn in a monolingual English classroom except that it is learned through two languages and includes consideration for the cultural heritage of both groups of students. Students in a bilingual classroom, like other students, are provided instruction in language skills, science, social studies, history, music, art, and physical education.

These subjects are the same basic subjects provided children in an all-English language program. How, then, does the bilingual dimension enter the picture? Is the school day extended? Do any of the subjects suffer from inadequate treatment? To answer these questions, curriculum writers have suggested or have come up with schedules of their own. A sample daily schedule for a bilingual program involving Spanish-dominant and English-dominant students with a self-contained bilingual teacher is proposed by Saville and Troike (see Figure 1, p. 12). Reporting on the diversity of scheduling patterns operating in Chicago, Reyes identifies six basic types (see Figures 2-7, pp. 13-16).

The San Francisco Unified School District (1974) provides a typical schedule for its English/Chinese bilingual program where two teachers are teamed. One teaches completely in Chinese and the other in English. Students divide their day as follows:

English Component	*Chinese Component*
1. English Language Arts (Listening, Speaking, Reading, Writing)	1. Chinese Language Arts (Listening, Speaking, Reading, Writing)
2. Spoken English	2. Spoken Cantonese

Figure 1

Sample Daily Schedule — Reciprocal

(Saville and Troike, 1971)

	Group A	Group B
11:00-11:30	Handwriting with aide	Science with teacher in English
11:30-12:30	Lunch	
12:30-1:00	Social Studies with teacher in Spanish	SSL (reinforcement of concepts in second language with aide) while practicing new language patterns
1:00-1:30	ESL (reinforcement of concepts in second language with aide) while practicing new language patterns	Social Studies with teacher in English
1:30-2:30	Art, Music, Literature	

	Group A	Group B
8:00-8:20	Opening activities (Spanish one week, English the next)	
8:20-8:45	Reading group with teacher in Spanish	Seat work supervised by aide, work on letter names, or other activities developing reading skills in English
8:45-9:00	Seat work supervised by aide, work on letter names, or other activities developing reading skills, in Spanish	Reading group with teacher in English
9:00-9:10	Break	
9:10-9:30	English as a Second Language (ESL)	Spanish as a Second Language (SSL)
9:30-10:00	Arithmetic in English or in Span	
10:00-10:30	Physical Education	
10:30-11:00	Science with teacher in Spanish	Handwriting with aide

Figure 2

Departmentalized Segregated Full Day Transitional Program

(Reyes, 1975)

A	Grade 6	B
1. Bilingual English-Dominant Teacher (Board Funded) 21 Spanish-Dominant Students--Advanced in English English Language Arts, Mathematics, Art in English	Students Change Classes ⟷	1. Bl/Bc Spanish Dominant Teacher 25 Spanish-Dominant Students--Beginners in English Spanish Language Arts, Social Studies, Health in Spanish
A teacher comes to each class twice a week to teach science. Another teacher teaches music once a week to each class and also tutors math, and English language arts.		
Grades 7 and 8 follow the same pattern as the above.		

Figure 3

Self-Contained Segregated Full Day Transitional Program*

(Reyes, 1975)

Grade Six	1 Classroom 1 Bl/Bc Teacher Spanish-Dominant Teaching all subjects in Spanish except one period daily of E.S.L. 25 Spanish-Dominant Students
Grades 7 and 8 follow the same structure	

* *A major weakness of this design is the complete isolation of the Spanish-dominant student with a Spanish-dominant teacher.*

Figure 4

Team-Teaching Partially Integrated Full Day Program

(Reyes, 1975)

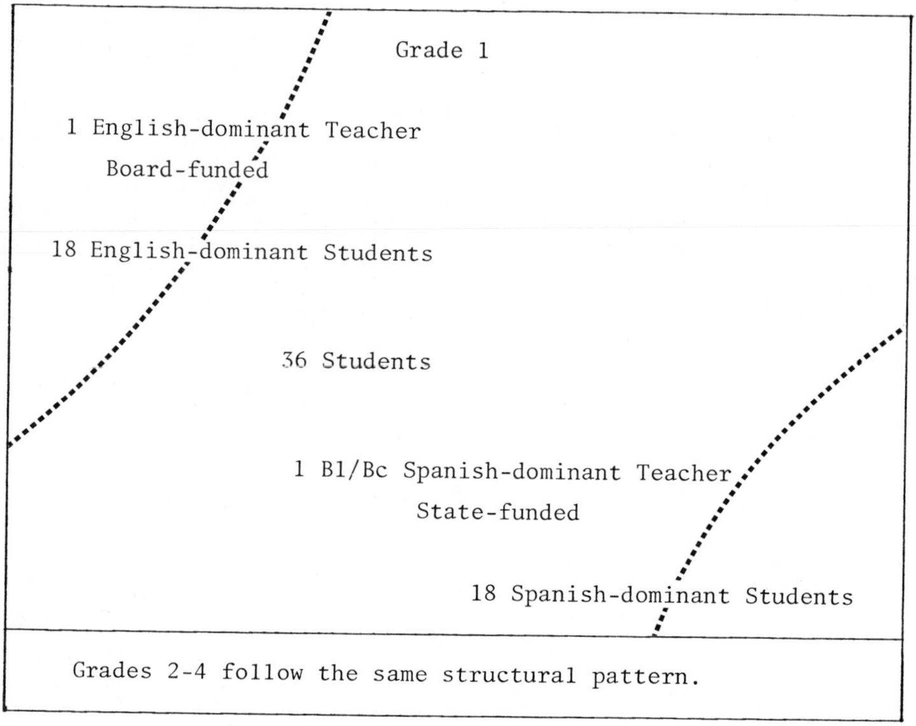

English-dominant Teacher teaches:

English Language Arts (English as a first language), English as a Second Language to Spanish-dominant students, Mathematics, Science, Social Studies in English.

Spanish-dominant Teacher teaches:

Spanish Language Arts (Spanish as a first language), Spanish as a Second Language, Social Studies in Spanish, Science and Math reinforcement in Spanish.

Physical Education, Art, Music--Integrated

Figure 5

Departmentalized Partially-Integrated Full Day

(Reyes, 1975)

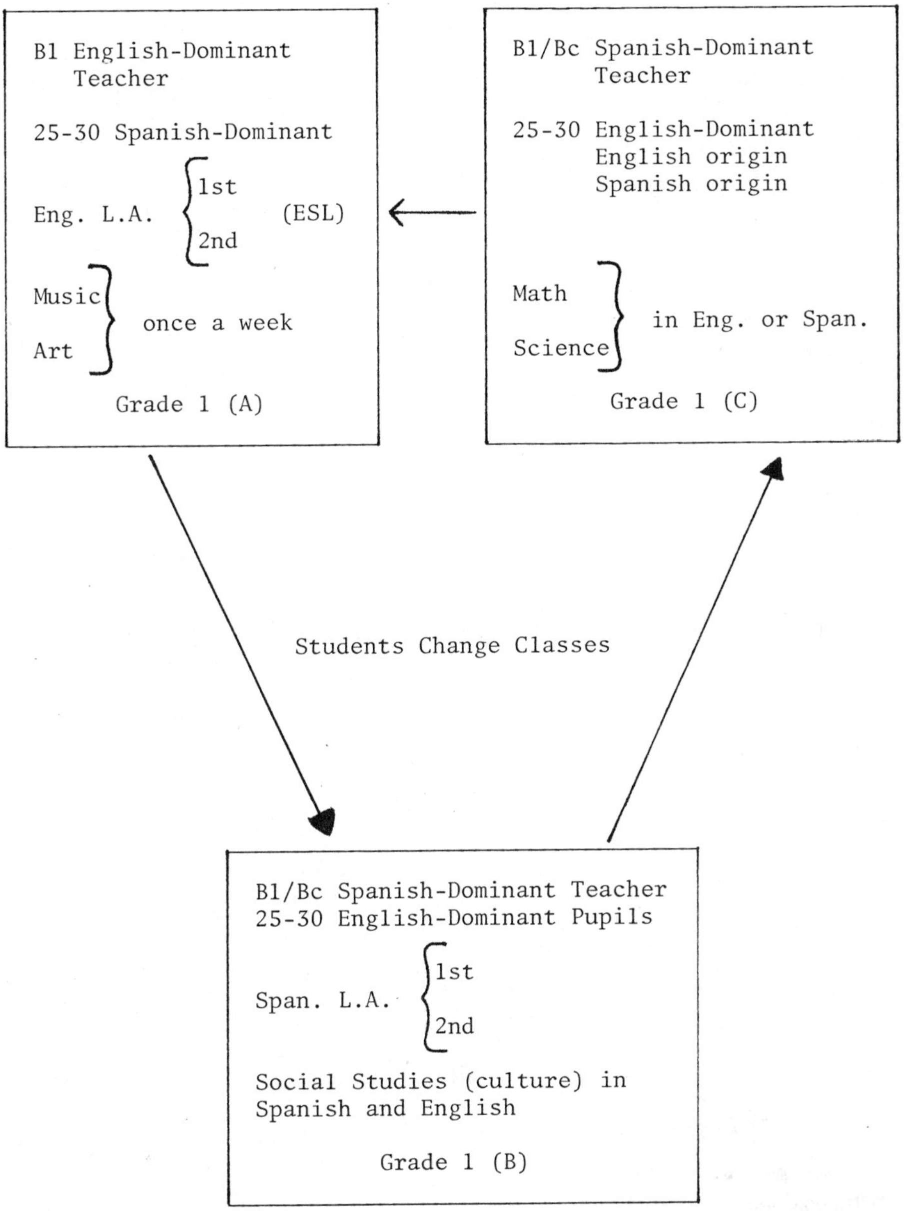

Figure 6

Pull-Out Half Day

(Reyes, 1975)

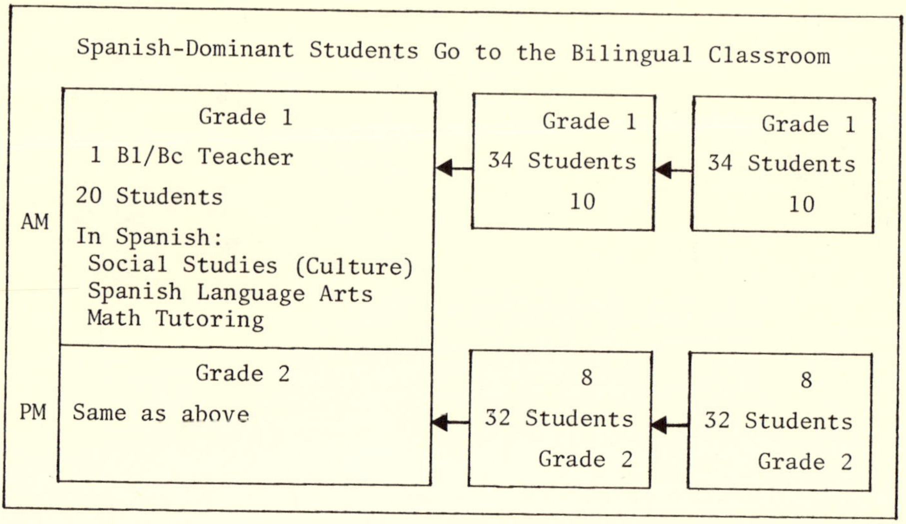

Figure 7

Team-Teaching Half Day

(Reyes, 1975)

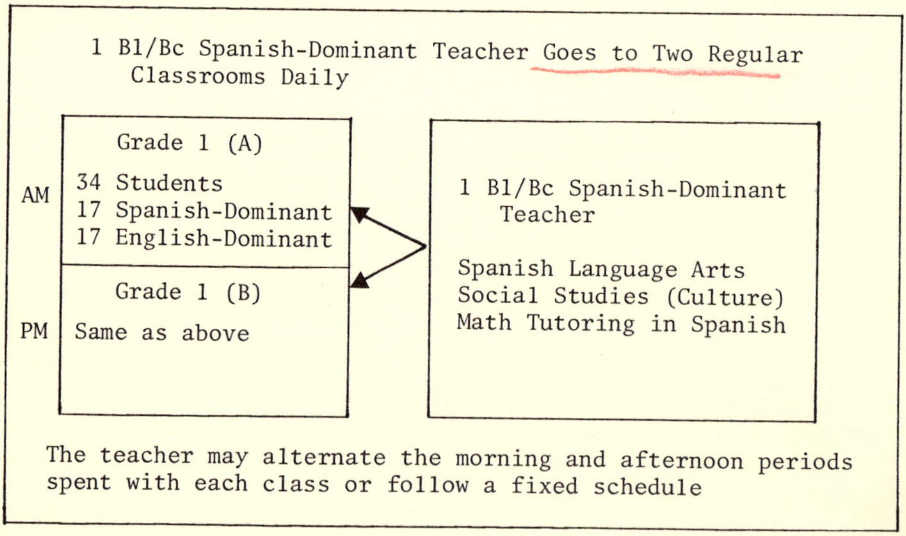

English Component	*Chinese Component*
3. Physical Education	3. Math
	4. Social Studies
	5. Science

This program would apply to Chinese-dominant children in grade one. The above schedules are by no means presented as intrinsically ideal. Rather, they have been designed to meet the needs of school districts with certain resources and student population characteristics. These schedules show that educators who are serious about bilingual education have incorporated this dual-language teaching approach into the basic program of studies. They substantiate the suggestion made by Ulibarrí (1970) that bilingual education should be an integral part of the overall education process and not an appendage.

Languages of Instruction

The overwhelming majority of bilingual education programs involve English and Spanish as languages of instruction. This comes as no surprise to anyone in view of the latest survey of languages other than English spoken in the United States (Waggoner, 1976). In July 1975 there were an estimated 25,334,000 persons in the United States living in households where languages other than English are spoken. A breakdown follows (Waggoner, 1976):

Figure 8

Languages	*No. of Speakers*
Spanish	8.2 million
Italian	1.8 million
German	1.5 million
French	1.5 million
Chinese, Greek, Japanese, Philippine languages, Portuguese, Korean	100,000-500,000 each

The rapid growth of the U.S. Spanish speaking population,

particularly in the Southwest and in large urban centers such as New York, Chicago, Miami and Seattle, has brought about almost an automatic equating of bilingual programs with the Spanish language. According to the Dissemination and Assessment Center for Bilingual Education (DACBE, 1975-1976), 284 of the 406 projects funded under Title VII dealt with the Spanish language. The remainder involved 46 other specific languages, including Arabic, Chinese, Choctaw, Hebrew, Portuguese, Russian, Vietnamese, Yaqui and Yup'ik.

This linguistic diversity underscores the pluralistic makeup of the country which has only recently come to be valued. Even though the overriding features of bilingual education today are compensatory or transitional in nature, the recognition of languages other than English can be seen as a step forward. The very fact that the large number of languages has survived within these shores clearly indicates the strong desire for belonging, for identification and for comfort from one's own kind. The 406 Title VII bilingual programs in 1975-1976 are a far cry from the first year of funding.

Table 1

Yearly Total of Projects, Children and Languages in Bilingual Education Projects

(DACBE, 1969-1976)

No. of Projects	*Year*	*No. of Students*	*No. of Languages*
76	1968-69*	33,732	14
63	1969-70	22,802	14
137	1970-71	45,227	16
169	1971-72	63,324	16
216	1972-73	100,391	24
211	1973-74	128,767	30
271	1974-75	147,523	34
406	1975-76	206,452	47

**Figures obtained from files of the National Consortium for Bilingual Education*

Although federal funding through ESEA Title VII has provided the necessary impetus to further the implementation of bilingual education programs, efforts at the local and state levels should be duly recognized. Descriptive information at these levels is scarce. One praiseworthy local effort, however, is discussed in the section "Implementing the Bilingual Program."

State legislation has, of course, increased the number

of bilingual education programs other than those supported by Title VII. At the time of this writing, there is no information concerning the number and extent of such non-federally funded programs. Nonetheless, the increase in the number of programs funded by the federal government, of students and of languages represented again shows the support in America for a pluralistic society. This pluralism, of which bilingual education is a vivid exponent, appears to have "caught on." In 1970, the Texas Education Agency came forward with its concept of "Confluence of Texan Cultures (1970)." In developing the plan to implement the concept into curriculum planning, the Texas State Board of Education not only recognized the cultural and linguistic diversity of the state, but encouraged schools to capitalize on the language and cultural strengths which all children bring to school. The concept of pluralism is also endorsed by the Council of Chief State School Officers (1977): "The Council believes that the development of an understanding and acceptance of cultural, language, and lifestyle differences among people should be an integral part of the instructional program for every student."

Foreign language educators are also rallying to the support of the pluralistic concept by encouraging their teachers to emphasize the non-English languages spoken in the U.S. The Northeast Conference on the Teaching of Foreign Languages devotes one entire issue of its *Reports of the Working Committees* (1976) to cultural pluralism and to the contributions to the United States of such linguistic groups as the French, Germans and the Spanish speaking. Other writers have made statements supporting a close relationship between bilingual education and the foreign language teaching field (Gaarder, 1975; Blanco, 1976).

Levels of Instruction

The Bilingual Education Act of 1968 as amended in 1974 does not necessarily limit its scope to the elementary school; yet, instruction in the elementary school is strongly emphasized in the wording of the Act. Section 702 uses the terms "child" and "children" nine times in identifying the target audience. The same section, however, provides financial assistance "...to enable local educational agencies to develop and carry out such [bilingual] programs in elementary and secondary schools (P.L. 93-380)." Schools have seen the greatest need for bilingual education at the preschool and the elementary school levels, since this is where the greatest concentration of children of limited English speaking ability is found. Of the 406 Title VII programs in 1975-76, only 83 were in grades nine through twelve (DACBE, 1975-76). Programs at these grade levels are usually reserved for students who have recently immigrated to this country and are commonly found in such urban centers as New York, Seattle, Boston, San Francisco and Chicago. Other secondary programs are designed for students whose command of English does not allow them to participate fully in the all-English instructional program.

Adult bilingual education programs are relatively few. Although there has not been a great deal of activity in the field of adult education, the Education Service Center in Texas has published materials in this field. The materials consist of three volumes and their purpose is to show schools how to build on the skills and concepts known to the learner in his language and how to make a smooth transition into the English language. The materials deal with the Mexican American and include information on the following topics (ESC, 1976): (a) formal and informal placement procedures and instruments, (b) structure of an adult education bilingual program, (c) staff development, (d) sections on Spanish phonology, vocabulary and grammatical structure and (e) sections on science, mathematics, social studies, culture, reading and writing in Spanish and English. Although the intent of the materials is to make a transition into English, they are not solely concerned with the teaching of English as a second language. The materials do address the teaching of subject matter in both Spanish and English.

IMPLEMENTING THE BILINGUAL PROGRAM

Needs Assessment

Needs assessment may be divided into three major categories: (a) determining need, (b) identifying students and their entry-level skills and (c) identifying resources. Andersson and Boyer (1970) urge school boards to establish a study committee to determine the feasibility of bilingual education. This, of course, assumes that the school board is already predisposed to consider a program. The State Education Department of New York (1972) recommends a community inventory in which the school undertakes a survey to determine the (a) languages spoken, (b) goals desired by the community, (c) ongoing programs related to language instruction, i.e. foreign language programs and (d) school resources.

What if the board or the administration does not even wish to consider the issue? Although the need for a bilingual program may seem outwardly obvious, local politics may dictate the strategies to be taken in identifying the needs. In Wilmington, DE there was no bilingual education program in 1973, and the ESL program had been discontinued on the grounds that there was an insufficient number of students to warrant the program. The truth was that this particular high school had 93 Puerto Rican students, 33 of whom could not function adequately in a regular English language classroom. Waserstein (1975) reports on the following procedures used in establishing the Wilmington Bilingual Education Program.

1. Obtained information from students, teachers, and administrators by asking them to verbalize their complaints and to indicate the resources they needed.
2. Worked closely with community representatives and disseminated information in English and Spanish about the progress of the effort.
3. Formed a negotiating team which included community representatives.
4. Held regular meetings to define strategies of the forthcoming negotiations with the school administration.
5. Attended social functions of the Puerto Rican community to provide additional visibility and information.
6. Visited established bilingual programs in other cities and used them as models.
7. Established continuing contact with key school personnel.
8. Persisted in carrying out the goal of establishing the bilingual program.

Communities located in states with bilingual education legislation are obligated to establish bilingual programs where a minimum number of children with limited or no command of the English language are identified. In Texas, for example, local schools must establish bilingual programs if they have "...an enrollment of 20 or more children of limited English-speaking ability in any language classification in the same grade level during the preceeding scholastic year ...(Texas S.B. 121, Sec. 21.453)." The Texas Education Agency places the onus of identifying children of limited English speaking ability (LESA) on the local schools. The method of identifying LESA children and of determining their dominant language is a critical issue in bilingual education today. Central to this issue is the very concept of bilingualism. Macnamara (1967) defines "bilingual" as an individual who possesses even a minimal degree of proficiency in at least one of the four language skills (listening, speaking, reading, writing). The person who could read a second language with little direct comprehension would qualify as bilingual, according to Macnamara.

The task facing teachers and administrators, however, is much more complex. Legislation asks schools to identify LESA children and to provide instruction in their stronger, or dominant, language. On the surface, it would appear that determination of language dominance would be a relatively simple matter: Either a person is monolingual, a "balanced" bilingual (equally proficient in two languages) or he has a better command of one language than the other. The simplistic view of bilingualism which assumes that the bilingual can express anything and everything in both languages has been responsible for many of the woes faced by individuals who have used a language other than English in the home and are suddenly asked to perform a task in the language which has not been used for that particular purpose. For example, an individual may speak Portuguese at home, but when describing the parts of a car in the home language, his terminology in this language may be limited. Halliday (1968) states that bilingualism tends to become specialized, since few individuals who have learned two languages from childhood rarely perform all language activities in both.

If not put into context, the question of bilingualism may get out of hand by assuming that all Mexican American children or those who have a Spanish surname, for example, are automatically bilingual or are monolingual in Spanish. Schools, therefore, are charged with one or both responsibilities for (a) systematically identifying the children's stronger or dominant language for placement purposes and/or (b) providing the teacher with information regarding the nature of children's linguistic repertoire for diagnostic and, subsequently, instructional purposes.

Most bilingual education programs are concerned with assessment of children's aural-oral abilities since this procedure is undertaken prior to reading-writing instruction. A matrix for each of the bilingual's languages is proposed by Macnamara (1967) which includes all four language skills.

Table 2

Matrix of Four Aspects of Each of the Four Major Language Skills

Encoding		*Decoding*	
Speaking	Writing	Listening	Reading
Semantics	Semantics	Semantics	Semantics
Syntax	Syntax	Syntax	Syntax
Lexicon	Lexicon	Lexicon	Lexicon
Phonemes	Graphemes	Phonemes	Graphemes

Zirkel's matrix (1974) is somewhat more complex and adds the sociolinguistic dimensions of home, community and school along one axis, and culture along the axis representing the four language skills. These two writers simply point out the complexity of fully describing bilingualism in an individual. Language dominance instruments clearly cannot include all of these dimensions. The best that such tests can accomplish is to give the school some idea of a child's linguistic ability at a particular time. It would be up to the school to extrapolate or predict the child's linguistic competence from the relatively meager information provided by the test.

Writers also differ as to the method of determining language dominance. Zirkel (1974) prefers to base language dominance on aural ability, simply because an aural-oral test requires individual administration and, often, trained scorers. Matluck and Mace (1973) remind us, however, that effective instruments should measure both the child's receptive and productive abilities. They make two further recommendations: The method of testing must be appropriate for the young child and the length of the test should be within the range that the child can perform productively.

Another issue involves the use of structured versus unstructured tests. Dickson (1975) points out that unstructured tests or free conversation allows the student to use the full range of his linguistic repertoire. The objection to this approach is that the success of the test depends on the skill of the tester and the mood and interests of the child. Structured tests require the child to respond to a series of predetermined commands and questions. Obviously, an argument against this approach is that it limits the child. The majority of language dominance tests are, however, structured since tests of this nature are easier to administer and score, and the realiability factor is easier to maintain.

Appendix A provides a list of language dominance tests and language proficiency tests. The line between these two categories is often a fine one and some aspects of the language dominance tests could be used as diagnostic measures and as indicators of language proficiency. Generally, proficiency tests provide linguistic information which may be used diagnostically. Although the tests' designers have constructed the instruments with certain goals or purposes in mind, in the final analysis, it is the school which determines the ultimate use of the tests and the benefits to be derived from the resulting information.

As was pointed out earlier, the procedure for determining a bilingual child's dominant language is still inexact. Both Zirkel (1974) and Halliday (1968) would agree that the variables of topic, place and audience may influence a person's behavior at any particular time. For this reason, once a child is categorized as being dominant in a particular language, the school should provide every opportunity to revise this judgment, based on the teacher's further observation over a period of time and on information from his parents about the child's language behavior outside the classroom.

In addition to identifying the child's linguistic strengths, the school should have some sort of assessment or degree of understanding of the child's basic concepts in social studies, science and arithmetic. Valencia (1972) suggests using *Tests of Basic Experiences* (Moss, 1970) to ascertain knowledge in several areas, using the Spanish language. This test also provides a Spanish language measure with particular reference to children in the early grades.

Writers in the field of bilingual education warn against the use of norm-referenced or standardized tests with minority group children (USCCR, 1975; Christian and Sharp, 1972; Balinsky and Peng, 1974; Bernal, 1972; DeAvila and Hanassy, 1974). Standardized tests reflect experiences which are often not known to minority children. These cultural biases may place minority children at a disadvantage and the tests would not be valid in terms of indicating the skills and knowledge they possess. Obviously, a child who grew up in rural Texas could hardly be expected to identify a picture of a sled or a high-rise apartment complex such as those found in Chicago or New York. The reverse is also true. The urban child from the North may have never seen an orange grove or a field of cotton. Bernadoni (n.d.) states that if a school has to use standardized tests (perhaps because of school policy), the testing should be done by trained personnel cognizant of the many limitations of tests for bicultural students. Indiscriminate testing, he warns, may result in inaccurate assessment and consequently in erroneous labeling and placement of children.

Ramírez and Castañeda (1974) feel that different intellectual patterns among Chinese, Jewish, Black and Puerto Rican children are the result of culturally determined learning styles. They go on to state that their research generally indicates that Mexican American children tended toward a field-dependent cognitive style--their mode of perception is such that "the organization of the field as a whole dominates perception of its parts." Such children perform best on verbal tasks of I.Q. tests; they learn materials more easily which have a social content; they are sensitive to the opinions of others and they react favorably when authority figures are confident of their ability. Field-independent children, on the other hand, perform well on analytic tasks; they learn material more easily that is impersonal and their performance is not greatly affected by the opinions of others. These views have not been conclusively proved. However, educators would do well to study the implications of this research for possible effects on the instruction of minority children.

Another dimension of assessment which is vital to the program is the identification of resources necessary for implementation. These can be categorized into three areas: finances, personnel and materials. Although it goes without saying that the teacher is the key to any type of successful instructional program, the other two elements are also necessary. Title VII has provided local school districts with funds for program implementation with the idea that, once the federal monies are no longer forthcoming, the local school district will make the commitment of taking over the financial support. In identifying financial resources, a school must decide if federal funds are to be requested and the amount of local support available for the proposed bilingual program. Funds for an instructional supervisor and support personnel, in-service training of personnel and instructional materials (textbooks, audio-visual materials and equipment and testing instruments) are considered essential.

The identification and utilization of personnel--especially teachers--constitute the most important elements in determining available resources. Obviously, teachers with a good command of the non-English language are essential to the success of the program. With the Title VII 1974 amendments, institutions of higher education became eligible to request funds for teacher training programs. Prior to that time, local schools relied on in-service training for preparing their bilingual teachers. Before a school district begins a bilingual education program, it must take stock of its teachers who are capable of instruction in the non-English language.

The school district should be aware of the kinds of instructional materials which are available. In some cases, the school district furnishes textbooks and in others the state provides schools with basic books. School districts should also be informed about the type of teaching materials available through the federally funded materials development centers and through the Dissemination and Assessment Center for Bilingual Education. It is sufficient to say at this point that the local school, in determining its needs and identifying available resources, should be knowledgeable about the materials which have been developed for students and teachers. In addition to having teaching skills and knowledge of subject matter required of regular teachers, the bilingual education teacher must also have a thorough knowledge of English and the other language of the bilingual program. The administration, in identifying its teaching personnel, should go beyond a simplistic approach which assumes that a member of a minority group automatically has all of the linguistic skills and cultural knowledge required to carry out an effective bilingual instruction program. The school district must be prepared to provide its teachers with an on-going program which addresses their needs.

Thus, it can be seen that the need for a bilingual program is based on proper identification of LESA children. This identification should be carried out as much as possible in a systematic manner using formal language assessment instruments, parental judgment and later, teacher judgment. Proper program planning and implementation also require assessment of the school district's needs in terms of finances, personnel and materials. Needs assessment must be an on-going process which keeps both teachers and administrators abreast of the latest developments in the program and allows for continual program revision.

Administration

Relatively little has been written concerning the role of the administrator in a bilingual education program. The role of the teacher, as the director and implementer of the instructional phase of the program, is paramount to the success of the program. Yet it is the leadership of the school superintendent, the campus principals and the bilingual program director which makes available to the teacher the facilities, finances, materials and moral support to carry out an effective instructional program.

In establishing a bilingual program, Andersson and Boyer (1970) stress the importance of the program coordinator or director. They indicate that the coordinator's basic responsibilities are to implement the policy determined by the school board and to assist in the recruitment of other personnel--teachers, teacher aides, specialists in curriculum design, materials development and evaluation, librarians, counselors and public relations specialists. Andersson and Boyer also indicate some characteristics or skills which the coordinator should have. Foremost in their recommendations is that the individual be a bilingual educator. By this they mean that the person selected for this key position be either a native speaker of the target language of the community with good control of English, or a native speaker of English with a good command of the other language. Andersson and Boyer also cite a sympathetic understanding of the culture of the target population and public relations skills as important. In terms of the coordinator's training, they suggest work in the fields of sociology, linguistics, anthropology and psychology. Language should be added to these fields--formal, in-depth study *in* the target language, as contrasted with linguistics which involves theoretical and applied study *about* language.

Given the relatively recent introduction of bilingual education into the curriculum, many programs employ teachers or administrators from the target population who may have varying levels of experience with bilingual education. Institutions of higher education are just now beginning to produce specialists in bilingual education at the undergraduate and graduate levels. These specialists will probably come closer to possessing competencies in the recommended areas than those individuals without university training. It would seem reasonable, moreover, that the director of a bilingual education program possess the knowledge and skills required of the bilingual classroom teacher whom he is to supervise and direct. The competencies outlined in *Guidelines for the Preparation and Certification of Teachers of Bilingual/Bicultural Education* (Center for Applied Linguistics, 1974) are most appropriate for the director of a bilingual education program.

The areas covered by these competencies go beyond those suggested by Andersson and Boyer for the bilingual coordinator. The Center's teacher competencies deal with the following areas: language proficiency, linguistics, culture, instructional methods, curriculum utilization and adaptation, assessment, school-community relations and supervised teaching. Not only must the bilingual director have competence in these areas, but he must be at a level which will allow him to carry out his role of both leader and agent of change for the bilingual program.

Although the literature contains much information about the components of a bilingual program, the duties of the director are implied rather than explicitly stated. Reference is often made to such concerns as language assessment, but it is usually assumed that the teacher will take the major responsibility in this phase. It is also assumed that it is the teacher who identifies, examines and orders the assessment instruments. It goes without saying that the program director should also have a major supportive role in this particular process. Again, we refer to Andersson and Boyer (1970) for suggestions about the responsibilities of the bilingual director or coordinator:

1. Implement the basic policy established by the school board.
2. Plan, with the teaching staff, the bilingual program.
3. Propose improvements in the program.
4. Recruit bilingual teachers, teacher aides, specialists in curriculum design, materials development, and evaluation.
5. Coordinate the preparation of materials based on the lore of the target group.

6. Serve as a liaison with the news media and the community to disseminate information about the bilingual program.
7. Coordinate the parental involvement effort.
8. Provide an effective in-service program for the staff.

To these duties one should add the following.

9. Keep abreast of the latest developments in bilingual education through research and professional meetings.
10. Keep superiors and the school board abreast of the status of the bilingual program.
11. Assist in the supervision and evaluation of the bilingual teaching personnel.
12. Serve as a public relations person with the campus principals.

The role of the bilingual director, as the foregoing implies, is vital to the success of the program. The importance of the coordinator is also upheld by Waserstein (1975), who pressed for the appointment of an interim part-time administrator until a permanent bilingual director was named for the Wilmington (Delaware) public schools. Since this particular bilingual program was begun because of pressure from outside the school, Waserstein feels that the appointment of an interim coordinator had a psychological effect on the administration "...once the temporary coordinator was hired, this became 'their' program and things began to move a little smoothly."

Although the bilingual director plays the principal administrative role in the bilingual program, other key administrators should be an integral part of the program. Visible support of and interest in the program are elements which can go far in the program's success. Ballesteros (1976) reports that 76 percent of the school principals involved in his study agreed that a bilingual education program is an effective way of teaching non-English speaking Mexican American children. Fifty-five percent agreed that bilingual children should spend a portion of the day learning in their native language and the remainder learning in English. He also reports that 71 percent of the principals agreed that bilingual education fosters improvement in the self-concept of the Spanish speaking student. Such positive attitudes can go far in fostering goodwill among the faculty and this, in turn, will affect the instructional program in a positive manner. A good example of administrative support was demonstrated by Superintendent Harold Brantley of the United

Independent School District of Laredo, Texas. Through his efforts, this pioneer program was initiated in 1964 and is still flourishing, which is indicative of the psychological effect of administrative support. Although not all upper echelon administrators have been responsible for the initiation of their bilingual programs, they can provide support by (a) holding regular meetings with the bilingual coordinator to keep apprised of the progress of the program and of bilingual education in general, (b) keeping the school board current and indicating support of the program, (c) visiting classrooms and talking to teachers about the program and (d) attending professional meetings dealing with bilingual education. The effective administration of the bilingual program and the concomitant support which it implies, therefore, forms the framework within which the instructional activities function.

Classroom Management

Effective utilization of resources is necessary for the implementation of a bilingual program. Gonzales and Lezama (1973) report on a dual language model of bilingual education which utilizes a team-teaching approach. Their program teams two teachers within the same classroom. One teaches only in Spanish and the other only in English. This arrangement solves the problem of how to keep the two languages separate. "[C]hildren are exposed to a language consistently by one individual and they will come to associate that individual as both an ethnic and language representative." Despite the educational benefits of such an arrangement, it is immediately obvious that the cost of providing two teachers for the same classroom may discourage administrators from adopting it. However, in a large open classroom which houses two or more classes, this arrangement would prove more economical.

Barrera (n.d.) has come forth with several plans, one of which recommends the teaming of monolingual English teachers with bilingual teachers in their classrooms. The program shown in Table 3 (p. 30) is designed for bilinguals and monolinguals in English and Spanish. It should be noted that a team-teaching arrangement of this type is desirable because it has the potential of providing students with a clear separation of the two languages and because it utilizes all teachers, whether they are bilingual or not.

An important element which is extremely helpful in effective classroom management is a teacher's aide, since the teacher is often responsible for dual language instruction. Pratt and Ramey (1974) recommend that teachers' aides assist by (a) counseling students, (b) serving as a liaison with the community and (c) assisting in instruction--provide reinforcement to concepts presented by the teacher. Other writers (Krear and Voci, 1972; LaFontaine, 1971; C.V. Pérez,

Table 3

Teamed Classrooms, Bilingual and Non-Bilingual Teachers
(Barrera, n.d.)

<table>
<tr><th>Subject Matter</th><th>Bilingual Teacher</th><th>Non-Bilingual Teacher</th></tr>
<tr><td>Spanish-English Language Arts
(30 minutes at early stages; 45 minutes when children begin reading in either language)
(55 minutes)</td><td>Teaches Spanish as a second language to English monolinguals and Spanish language arts to bilinguals.
Teaches Spanish monolinguals Spanish language arts (native language instruction) and Spanish language arts to bilingual students.</td><td>Teaches English as a second language to Spanish monolinguals and English language arts to bilinguals.
Teaches English monolinguals English language arts (native language instruction) and English language arts to bilingual students.</td></tr>
<tr><td rowspan="2">Math
(35 minutes)</td><td>Teaches math in Spanish to Spanish-dominant students and bilinguals.
Alternative: Four days in Spanish and one day vocabulary drill in English.</td><td>Teaches math in English to English-dominant students and bilinguals.
Alternative: Four days in English and one day vocabulary drill in Spanish.</td></tr>
<tr><td colspan="2">Alternative: Follow preceding plan, but individualized and use either language depending on child's language dominance.</td></tr>
<tr><td rowspan="3">Social Studies
(55 minutes)</td><td>Teaches in Spanish to Spanish monolinguals.</td><td>Teaches in English to English monolinguals.</td></tr>
<tr><td colspan="2">Both teachers teach one unit in Spanish and one in English (not on the same subject) to bilinguals.</td></tr>
<tr><td>Alternative: Four days in Spanish and one day in vocabulary drill in English.</td><td>Alternative: Four days in English and one day in vocabulary drill in Spanish.</td></tr>
<tr><td>Cultural Activities
(25 minutes)</td><td colspan="2">Music in both languages. Art instructions provided in both languages reflecting both cultures. Dances of cultures represented.</td></tr>
</table>

1971) have suggested additional roles for teachers' aides, such as assisting the teacher in materials development; communicating with the non-English speaking child; supervising children in the cafeteria, playground, etc.; telling stories to the children and taking care of instructional materials like books and audio-visuals. In essence the function of the aides is to release teachers from much of the routine work, so their time can be devoted to actual planning and instruction. From the psychological point of view, aides can be seen by the child as a link with the community, since in many cases aides may be neighbors. It should be stressed that the use of bilingual aides as the sole source for the non-English language should not be tolerated; this is a poor excuse for a "bilingual" program. Aides, though very valuable, cannot and should not be expected to carry out the instructional duties required by the teacher. Quality bilingual education cannot be a reality unless the program has the full support of an administration which is committed to providing children with competent bilingual teachers.

As suggested by Barrera (n.d.), English monolingual, Spanish monolingual and bilingual students can be brought into the bilingual program in an effective manner. Grouping of students *within* the classroom for some of the instruction is what she recommends. It is important, however, that all groups of children come in contact with each other for instructional purposes during specific portions of the day rather than being completely segregated. Not only is segregation of students by race, color or national origin for all instructional activities prohibited by Title VI of the 1964 Civil Rights Act (P.L. 88-352), but good educational practice allows children to learn from each other. To accomplish this, Valencia (1972) recommends the arrangements illustrated in Figures 9 and 10, found on page 32.

Figure 9 shows progression of the bilingual student toward all of the English language arts and a progression of the English monolingual toward all of the Spanish language arts. Both Valencia and Barrera make provisions to bring all students together during some portions of the day, including classes where cognitive development is not the primary goal, such as art, music and physical education. Figure 10 is an expansion of Section B in Figure 9. Grouping by language should be done only in cases where the first language keeps the child from participating in learning activities bilingually or in the second language.

One example of effective classroom management is in the Austin Independent School District, where learning centers and individualized instruction are combined. Classrooms are arranged so students move around three or four centers (including a listening center and a reading center), where the teacher, an aide or a student teacher assists them. Using contracts and skill boxes, reading is taught on an

Figure 9

Homogeneous Instruction and Movement Toward Heterogeneous Bilingual Instruction

(Valencia, 1972)

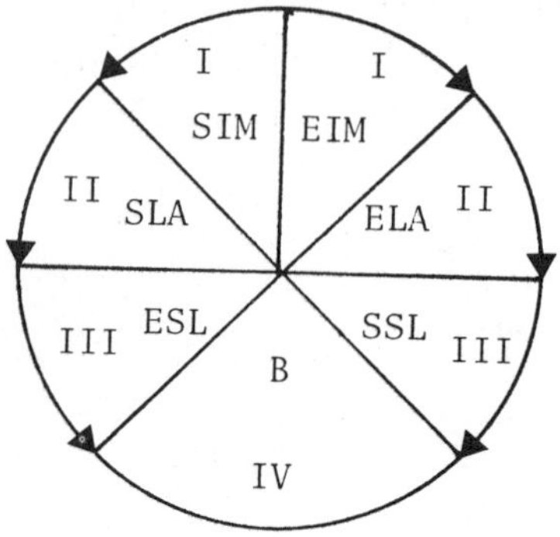

EIM = Eng Inst Med

SIM = Span Inst Med

ELA = Eng Lan Arts for Eng Speakers

SLA = Span Lang Arts for Span Speakers

ESL = Eng as a Sec Lang for non-Eng Speakers

SSL = Span as a Sec Lang for non-Span Speakers

B = Bilingual activities across various Subject Matter areas

Figure 10

Heterogeneous Bilingual Model

(Valencia, 1972)

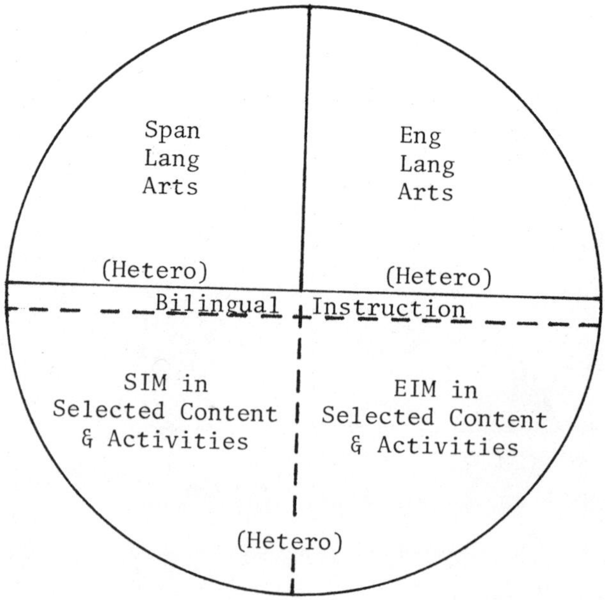

an individualized basis. Students work on their own for certain periods during the day and teachers or their assistants check the students' work. A timer signals a change of learning center when students work individually or in small groups of five to seven.

Methodology

As was indicated earlier, bilingual education should be considered an integral part of general education and there is nothing exotic or unusual about this form of education other than the use of two languages instead of one. As far as methodology in subjects such as social studies, science and math is concerned, the teacher should use the same methods as would be used with monolingual English speaking children. The difference, of course, is the treatment given to the two languages involved.

To illustrate this point, Sánchez (n.d.) presents some fundamental principles of modern mathematics which can be found in any program or set of materials regardless of language. Some of his main points are that (translated from Spanish by the present writer: (a) modern math seeks to develop the child's intuitive abilities, (b) modern math makes a distinction between the properties of cardinal and ordinal numbers, (c) emphasis is placed on a knowledge of the structure of the numbering system and of relative value, (d) the arbitrary nature of symbolism is fundamental to all the subject matter presented, (e) a great deal of geometry is included and (f) the concept of the set is treated extensively.

Sánchez goes on to mention that the use of math labs is gaining wide acceptability and that teacher training programs have been emphasizing the methodology involved with the new math. Glenadine Gibb (1974), immediate past president of the National Council of Teachers of Mathematics, expressed concern for the LESA child studying mathematics. She states that teachers should not only have the sensitivity to the student's needs in terms of cultural differences, but they should also speak the student's preferred language.

Saville and Troike (1971) take an opposite stand on the teaching of mathematics in the bilingual program: "Whatever the dominant language of the child, mathematical computational skills should first be developed in English since advanced work in mathematics will probably be done in this language and later switching of these skills is difficult."

The advisability of this recommendation is questionable, since the same might be said of other subjects in the curriculum. Furthermore, the teaching of math or any other subject in a language other than the child's dominant one goes against one of the basic tenets of education: "It is axiomatic that the best medium for teaching a child is in his mother tongue (UNESCO, 1955)." Pérez (1975) addresses the issue of instructional methods:

> Mastery of a variety of innovative teaching techniques and strategies and the ability to implement such through both languages are essential skills for the bilingual educator. A linguistically mixed classroom demands the utilization of techniques such as individualized instruction and the utilization of learning centers. The lack of proper training and familiarity with the process of implementation of these processes can result in occasional chaotic classroom situations where little is learned in either language.
>
> It is essential that bilingual teachers become expert classroom managers.

While the terms "bilingual methodology" and "bilingual teaching techniques" are widely used, there is really no indication of their existence. What turns out to be "methodology" is, in reality, the use of two languages in the instructional program. The issue becomes one of classroom management and the treatment of the languages of instruction is vital to the success of the program. The ratio of time devoted to the use of the two languages and the overall goals of the program, whether maintenance or transitional, would determine (to a large extent) the success or failure of the bilingual program. However, it should be pointed out that, if the research findings described earlier by Castañeda, Herold and Ramírez (1975) are valid, educators would do well to develop specialized methodologies geared to the needs of bilingual children who might have different learning styles from mainstream children.

Moving to the linguistic aspect of the curriculum, oral language development is seen as a vital yet often neglected part of the instructional program. Oral language assessment instruments are used to gain insights into the children's language competence. Yet, at times children are unable to understand what they read because of a limited vocabulary (Paulston, 1974). This situation occurs despite recommendations by curriculum planners to include oral language development as an integral part of the language arts program (Saville and Troike, 1971; Reyes, 1975). It can be argued that children are provided with oral language development as they participate in bilingual instruction in the various subject areas. By using language in a meaningful context, children can increase their command of both languages significantly. In this regard, however, teachers interested in increasing their students' oral command of the two languages should ask themselves: How much oral work is done in such subjects as social studies and science? What opportunities do children have to participate individually or by group in oral work? Compared to the children, what percentage of time does the teacher talk? Does work in subjects like social studies and science include linguistic (both cognitive and affective) objectives? Does the language arts component include opportunities to concentrate on difficult linguistic items through some type of pattern practice?

The key words in oral language development are *student participation*. In many instances, it is the teacher who does the majority of speaking and the children the greater part of listening. Some second language methodologists like Finocchiaro (1964) advocate the use of structured pattern practice. This methodology is an exponent of behavioristic psychology promoted by such individuals as Skinner (1957) and Carroll (1965) who view language learning as a process of habit formation learned by means of repetition and analogy. Correct responses are reinforced by praise or by the child's getting what he wants and incorrect responses are extinguished in the opposite manner. The child continues to imitate the language patterns of those around him and thus learns his first language. Applied to the classroom in first- or second-language lessons, the student is asked to repeat utterances and manipulate the language through pattern drills which are designed to help him internalize the language.

The other view of language learning supported by cognitive-code psychologists such as Chomsky (1966), Brown (1973) and Ervin-Tripp (1973) holds the notion that children are born with an innate capability for language acquisition. Language is not learned by imitation, practice and reinforcement; rather, as a child's cognitive ability develops, he uses increasingly more complex utterances. This view holds that the child hypothesizes about language and that he tests his language against what he hears; or he learns the rules of the language which he uses to create and understand sentences he has never heard. Classroom application of this view would require exposing the student to a maximum amount of natural language without reliance on pattern drills as in the behavioristic model. There is controversy concerning these two views of language learning.

In terms of second-language learning, some studies suggest that children use some of the same strategies in both first- and second-language acquisition (Milon, 1974; Natalicio and Natalicio, 1971). In their study on second-language acquisition, Dulay and Burt (1974) show that first-language interference accounts for a minimum of syntactic errors in children learning a second language. Furthermore, the study indicated that most of the syntactic errors in the children's second-language speech were indistinguishable from those in first-language acquisition.

Bilingual education teachers would do well to study the implications of both schools of thought, since the approaches associated with each seem to have merit. Although the teacher would not want to rely entirely on pattern practice and repetition, certainly some areas of difficulty can be identified for the purpose of intensive practice. Children should be given ample opportunities to use language in a great variety of situations that require actual communication with each other and adults. Because learning to read and write are among the primary goals of education, schools often do not give oral language development its rightful place in the curriculum. Since the ability to communicate orally usually precedes introduction to the reading and writing skills, the development of children's listening and speaking skills in two languages should be a primary concern for bilingual programs.

The teaching of subject matter in the home language and English is at the very core of bilingual education. We have already quoted the UNESCO axiom stating that the best language of instruction is the child's mother tongue. This procedure applies not only to the learning of such subject matter as social studies, arithmetic and science, but, according to some foreign language methodologists, also to the learning of reading (Brooks, 1960; Rivers, 1968; Finocchiaro, 1964). Such methodologists have supported the learning of the graphic skills in the second language only after the student has begun to understand and communicate in that language. The idea is that writing is a graphic representation of speech and that it must be present before the sound-symbol relationships are taught. In bilingual education, it is argued that the child should learn to read in his home or dominant language, since he has a command of its phonological and grammatical systems, and a sizable vocabulary. This was the premise of the study carried out by Modiano (1966) in Chiapas, Mexico. At the end of three years, the Indian children who had been taught to read in their mother tongue had higher reading comprehension than those who were taught to read in Spanish. Contradictory results were reported by Lambert and Tucker (1972) in the St. Lambert Experiment. In this study, monolingual English speaking children were taught only in French in kindergarten and grade one. English language skills were introduced in the second grade, but subject matter was presented in French through the fourth grade. This experimental group was compared to a monolingual French control group and to a monolingual English control group which had learned English as a second language and French as a second language, respectively. At the end of grade one, the experimental class was at the same level in French reading and word discrimination as the French control group. Although they had not been taught English reading, they scored at the 50th percentile on national norms for English speaking first grade children on tests of word knowledge and word discrimination and at the 15th percentile on reading skills. In the second grade, they were reading as well as either the French or English control groups, a level they maintained through the other grades.

Paulston (1974) feels one can draw tentative conclusions from the results of this study and from those provided by the Rizal Experiment (Philippines). She stresses the fact that learning to read involves two separate skills which are often confused in the literature. The first skill is concerned with learning the sound-symbol relationships and the second extracting lexical, syntactic and cultural meaning from the reading. She goes on to relate that she has seen Spanish speaking children in the second grade read a sentence like *Mi mamá me ama* and not understand it completely because the verb *amar* was not in their vocabulary. This situation is very similar to the statement made by bilingual education teachers, "They read beautifully, but they don't understand what they're reading."

Engle (1975) surveyed 24 studies which attempted to determine whether a child will learn to read more rapidly in a second language if he is first taught to read in his primary language. She concludes that most of the studies provided no substantial evidence as to which approach is better. Engle, however, points out that the variables in the studies were often not sufficiently controlled which significantly affected the results. She proposes 12 issues which should be taken into account in designing further research concerning language use in education:

1. The linguistic relationship between the two languages;
2. The functions of the two languages in the broader community, and the possible uses of literacy in each language;
3. The cultural context of learning in the community;
4. The relationship of the two ethnolinguistic groups in the large society;
5. The initial linguistic status of the child;
6. The period of the child's development in which the second language is introduced;
7. Instructional methods and materials used;
8. The ethnic group membership of the teacher;
9. The training and linguistic knowledge of the teacher;
10. The length of time necessary to observe an effect;
11. The specific subject matter under consideration;

12. The appropriateness of the assessment devices for both languages.

Although the studies reviewed by Engle did not reveal conclusive results concerning the teaching of reading in a child's first or second language, critics of bilingual education should not be too quick to dismiss this educational movement as unproductive. Much additional research is still needed to resolve such issues.

The issues concerning methodology in a bilingual program do not differ greatly from those found in monolingual programs. The question of language use and the incorporation of elements of the home culture into the instructional program are of prime concern and offer a point of departure from monolingual education.

Community Involvement

Nowhere in the overall school program is community or parental involvement as important as in the bilingual education program. While the young child may already feel that he is entering a strange world upon coming to school, a visible link with the home is indispensable to promote positive attitudes about the school. The National Education Association (NEA) has produced some publications designed to acquaint parents with their vital role in their children's education, and to show schools how to involve parents in the school program. One NEA pamphlet (n.d.), "Get Involved in your Child's School," suggests answers to: What is the parent involvement program and how does it benefit my child? Why do teachers need my help and do they really want me in the classroom? How can I help in the classroom? Another NEA publication (n.d.), "Parent-Teacher Relationships," advances the idea that the child does not come to the school alone once the parent is involved. The teacher may obtain a more accurate profile of the child by knowing the home conditions (such as family illness, economic problems or a happy event) which may affect school performance. Another NEA publication by Sayler (1971) gives schools guidelines on how to recruit and train parents to be partners in education. Some of the activities recommended for parents in the classroom include (a) preparing art materials, (b) assisting with outdoor play activities, (c) supervising the classroom while the teacher works with a small group in reading, (d) guiding creative writing table activities and (e) reviewing work with pupils.

One of the most important reasons for involving parents in the bilingual program is to use "...the cultural values and language of ethnic groups in the community...[so that] greater appreciation and understanding will promote positive feelings of self-worth and bicultural interaction (Smith and Caskey, 1972)." In this vein parents, grandparents and other members of the community may be brought in to relate stories, myths and poems, to sing songs and in general, to share with the children dimensions of the culture which might otherwise go untapped. The reality of the school incorporating elements of the home culture in the instructional program will go far in helping minority children to develop a positive self-image. On the other side of the coin, this type of involvement provides non-minority children with opportunities to experience first-hand cultural dimensions of their fellow classmates.

The use of parents in the instructional program or on school sites is one aspect of the community involvement component. There is the feeling that parents can help their children at home, too. One particular program, the Spanish Dame Bilingual Bicultural Project of San José, CA, established a model home-tutoring component (1975). This particular program aims to extend the school into the home through the use of tutors and parents trained to reinforce cognitive and psychomotor skills and concepts in the affective domain. The Spanish Dame Bilingual Bicultural Project has also come forth with another booklet (DACBE, 1974) which provides the tutor with concrete ideas and information concerning teaching techniques, daily lessons and a daily curriculum guide. These lessons, based on a language maintenance model, concentrate on such elements as language development, concept formation, perceptual development, motor skills, self-awareness, positive self-concept, health and safety, community and cultural awareness.

Bilingual Education Materials

The need for quality instructional materials has often posed serious problems for bilingual education programs. In the late 1960's, bilingual education programs relied on imported and teacher-made materials. Because of linguistic and cultural differences, teachers frequently found foreign materials difficult to use with children in this country. In the Southwest, for example, the children's Spanish dialect contained lexical items which were not used in the imported materials. Foreign materials used words like *habichuelas* for the child's familiar *frijoles*, *colmado* for *tienda*, and *chiringa* for *papalote* or *huila*. While these lexical differences represented linguistic diversity in the Spanish language, they were usually rejected in the Southwest by students and teachers alike. The number of unfamiliar words in the materials often proved discouraging to the students.

During this period federal funding under Title VII, ESEA, provided the necessary resources to establish the Materials Acquisition Project (Peña, 1973), which compiled the most comprehensive lists of commercial instructional materials available. The Dissemination Center for Bilingual Bicultural Education--now called the Dissemination and Assessment Center for Bilingual Education or DACBE, located in Austin, TX and also established through Title VII--sought to identify, edit, reproduce and distribute locally developed materials. The Center's publication, *Cartel*, provides annotated listings of commercially and noncommercially prepared materials.

Commercial publishers quickly recognized a market for bilingual education curriculum materials--particularly in Spanish. In some cases materials were prepared so hurriedly that speed became more important than quality. Some Spanish language materials were translations of English textbooks and often lacked cultural authenticity. While it is not the purpose of this paper to identify poor commercial materials nor to recommend quality commercial materials, local textbook committees, teachers and administrators are urged to evaluate materials being considered for purchase by using such instruments as the *EPIE Form A* (Educational Products Information Exchange Institute, 1976). Since this instrument, like any other, can only ask certain questions, the reviewer in the final analysis must possess an understanding of a variety of aspects of bilingual education and curriculum theory and practice. For example, if the reviewer has insufficient knowledge of a particular culture or language, it will be difficult to identify discrepancies in these areas.

The EPIE Institute has published two volumes which evaluate a large number of bilingual education materials. *Selector's Guide for Bilingual Education Materials, Vol. 1, Spanish Language Arts* (1976) and *Selector's Guide for Bilingual Education Materials, Vol. 2, Spanish "Branch" Programs* (1976) should serve teachers, curriculum planners and textbook selection committees to select the most appropriate Spanish language teaching materials for their programs. González (n.d.) has edited a handbook for assisting educators in reviewing materials for cultural relevancy. Among other things, the handbook provides valuable information concerning "formal" culture (art, literature, music) and "deep" culture (personal values, superstitions, behavior patterns). Through careful examination and analysis, local school personnel can determine the materials which best suit their program objectives.

Present Title VII legislation has made the establishment of nine materials development centers possible (DACBE, 1976). The purpose of these centers is to "develop instructional, teacher training, and testing materials in the languages and at the grade levels of the bilingual target groups being served." A brief description of the centers can be found in Table 4 on page 41.

As can be seen, the number of centers with responsibili-

Table 4

Materials Development Centers

(DACBE, 1976)

Center	*Materials*
Arizona Bilingual Materials Development Center (University of Arizona, Tucson)	Teacher training materials, grades K-3, Spanish.
Asian American Bilingual Center (Berkeley Unified School District)	Social studies, language arts, math, science, fine arts, grades PK-3, Cantonese, Philippino, Korean, Japanese, Lauwan; needs assessment, grades PK-3, Samoan.
Multilingual Multicultural Materials Development Center (California State Polytechnic University)	Social studies films and filmstrips, grades 7,8,9, Spanish; teacher's manuals, grades K-12, Spanish; language assessment instruments for teachers, grades K-12, Spanish.
Spanish Curricula Development Center (Dade County, FL, Public Schools)	Language arts, social studies, fine arts, Spanish, science, math (teacher's guides produced in Puerto Rican, Mexican American, Cuban and multi-ethnic editions will eventually encompass grades 1-6, Spanish); health (multi-ethnic teacher's guides only), grades 4-6, Spanish.
National Materials Development Center for French and Portuguese (New Hampshire College and University Council)	Subject areas as needed, K-6 (to be reviewed), grades K-12 and adult, French, Acadian French, Canadian French, Haitian French, Portuguese.
Native American Materials Development Center (Ramah Navajo School Board, Inc.)	Subject areas as needed, grades K-3, Native American languages.
Northeast Center for Curriculum Development (New York C.S.C. No. 7)	Social studies, language arts, fine arts, grades 1-9, Spanish; research, grades K-6, Greek, Italian, Haitian.
Bilingual Materials Development Center (Ft. Worth, TX, Independent School District)	Fine arts, Spanish and English communication skills, social studies, science, math, student materials, resource materials for teachers, teacher training materials, supportive materials and media, grades 6-9; ESL, grades 7-8; social studies, language arts, grade 6, French.
Midwest Materials Development Center (Milwaukee Board of School Directors)	Language arts, fine arts, social studies (cultural aspects emphasized), grades 4-6, Spanish.

ties in the Spanish language reflects the proportion of Spanish-English bilingual education programs in the nation. It is significant to note, however, that other languages such as Cantonese, Portuguese, Greek and Korean are included, since commercially prepared materials in these languages have not been forthcoming. The materials prepared by the centers, then, have played an important role in helping local schools implement bilingual programs in languages other than Spanish. The materials development centers also have met another need by producing materials in languages such as Spanish and French which represent a variety of dialects. These materials have helped to provide pupils with materials in a standard dialect which closely approximates their own home dialect. The illustrations and content are usually such that the children find them culturally familiar.

Another organization in materials preparation is the Southwest Educational Development Laboratory of Austin, TX which has developed a series of Spanish-English bilingual education materials. These materials include bilingual oral language and reading, Spanish reading, first grade social studies in Spanish, bilingual early childhood, bilingual kindergarten and bilingual continuous progress mathematics. These materials include teacher's manuals and teacher training materials.

Some commercial publishers which have translated materials from English into another language have not attempted to translate the teacher's manuals. It can be argued, of course, that the concepts are the same regardless of the language in which they are expressed and that the student materials are written in the target language. On the other hand, an opposite view can be argued from both psychological and linguistic perspectives. First, the fact that the teacher's manuals are in English places the target language in an inferior position: It is not sufficiently important to warrant its use in the teacher's materials. Secondly, the all-English manuals encourage the teacher to use the other language only when instruction takes place, but not in other situations. From a linguistic point of view, the use of the target language in the teacher's manuals increases exposure to this language, particularly as it concerns technical and pedagogical terminology. The Spanish-English materials produced by the Spanish Curricula Development Center are praiseworthy in this respect and serve as a model for other materials. The instructions to the teacher are provided in both languages and the teacher is thus provided with the opportunity of staying in the same language used to present the lesson.

Schools now have access to a variety of materials for teaching culture. Some that are being used are: (a) Bilingual Program ARRIBA, *Estudio cultural de Puerto Rico* (1973); (b) CANBBE Northeast Regional Adaptation Center, *Carteles puertorriqueños* (1973); (c) Bilingual Unit, New York State Department of Education, *Puerto Rican History, Civilization and Culture: a Mini-documentary* (1973); (d) Native American Materials Development Center, *Navajo Curriculum Series* (1976); and (e) Instructional Media Center, Alaska State-operated Schools, *Alaskan Folktales* (1976).

Of particular interest to teachers of Puerto Rican students are such resource materials as: (a) Matilde Colón Sánchez. *El bilingüismo en Puerto Rico y la actitud de un grupo de jóvenes bilingües hacia el idioma vernáculo.* Monograph #87, University of Puerto Rico, December 1972; (b) Israel Ramos Perea. "El ajuste escolar en los estudiantes migrantes--estudio piloto," Centro de Investigaciones Pedagógicas de la Universidad de Puerto Rico, *Boletín*, Vol. II, No. 1, 1 septiembre, 1970; and (c) Eduardo Seda Bonilla. "Cultural Pluralism and the Education of Puerto Rican Youths," *Phi Betta Kappan*, Vol. LIII, No. V, January 1972, pp. 294-96. A more extensive bibliography of such materials may be obtained from the Office of the Commonwealth of Puerto Rico (Votaw, 1976). These materials can be very useful to teachers, particularly in presenting folklore, history and customs of the groups indicated. Of interest, also, are the materials compiled by Marquevich and Spiegel, *Multiethnic Studies in the Elementary School Classroom* (1976), which provide valuable information about the folklore of Asian Americans, Eurasian Americans, Afro-Americans, Native Americans, Mexican Americans and Puerto Rican Americans.

With the influx of Vietnamese refugees and other Asian groups to this country, materials have been developed to assist schools in meeting the needs of these students. Of special note are: (a) Los Angeles Unified School District. *Bridging the Asian Language and Cultural Gap: A Handbook for Teachers* (1971-74); (b) The Center for Applied Linguistics. *A Handbook for Teachers of Vietnamese Students: Hints for Dealing with Cultural Differences in School* (1975); and (c) Lien Truong, Glendale Unified School District. *Counseling for Vietnamese Students* (n.d.).

Title VII has funded two dissemination and assessment centers: DACBE in Austin, TX and the Assessment and Dissemination Center at Fall River, located in Fall River, MA. The Massachusetts center edits, reproduces and distributes materials in Asian, French, Portuguese, Greek, Italian and Spanish. It should be mentioned that the seven resource centers funded by Title VII assist in training school personnel in the use of bilingual materials and field test the materials from the nine materials development centers. The three components--consisting of the seven resource centers, nine materials development centers and two dissemination and assessment centers--comprise the National Network for Bilingual Education (DACBE, 1976).

Professional literature for teachers in the area of

bilingual education is now coming into its own. To be sure, the manuals accompanying basic instructional materials are useful in suggesting teaching strategies for their respective textbooks. The dissemination and assessment centers have a number of good publications for professional growth and specific titles may be obtained through their respective catalogs.

Other materials useful for professional growth or initial teacher training include the classic two-volume work by Andersson and Boyer, *Bilingual Schooling in the United States* (1970), which provides a wealth of information about bilingual education from a national and international perspective, its history in the United States, a description of specific programs and curriculum models and a very extensive bibliography. Saville and Troike's *A Handbook of Bilingual Education* (1971) is useful from the point of view of providing the teacher with basic linguistic information, advice on the implementation of a bilingual program, the use of materials and community involvement. Litsinger's *The Challenge of Teaching Mexican American Students* (1973) may be of interest to teacher trainers preparing instructors for this particular cultural and linguistic group. It presents a historical perspective of the Mexican American, a rationale for bilingual-bicultural education and pedagogical suggestions for the teaching of subject matter in English and Spanish. The Texas Education Agency has developed a comprehensive training manual designed primarily for in-service education, *An Orientation to Bilingual Education in Texas: A Training Manual* (1976). This publication, which has been used widely in Texas, includes sections on materials utilization, parental involvement, oral language development, reading and classroom management. *New Approaches to Bilingual Bicultural Education* (1974), produced by Systems and Evaluations in Education, has consolidated a series of previously separate documents concerning the Mexican American. The publication includes chapters on pluralistic education, Mexican American values, learning styles, strategies for teaching the Mexican American and a self-assessment section for teachers to determine level of achievement after having read the book.

It is significant that professional journals are devoting their attention to issues in bilingual education. Noteworthy are *The Bilingual Review/La revista bilingüe* devoted exclusively to the study of bilingualism and bilingual education; *TESOL Quarterly*, which was originally designed to serve the needs of teachers of English to speakers of other languages, takes an avid interest in bilingual education; *Foreign Language Annals*, published by the American Council on the Teaching of Foreign Languages, regularly includes articles on language teaching as it relates to bilingual education; *Hispania*, the journal of the American Association of Teachers of Spanish and Portuguese, Inc., includes articles concerning the U.S. Spanish speaking population. This is not an all-inclusive list of resources for professional growth, but it does illustrate the numerous resources available to the bilingual teacher.

Program Evaluation

Curriculum planners (Tyler et al, 1968) distinguish between formative and summative evaluation. The first has to do with the determination of the effectiveness of the instructional program. Student progress is measured periodically to determine if the program objectives are being met. The information obtained is fed back into the program through the teachers so that interim program modifications may be made as needed. Although formal testing instruments can be used for this purpose, subjective information obtained through observation of student performance is used also. Summative evaluation is based on information provided by the formative evaluation process over an extended period of time. Its purpose is to determine the extent to which the program objectives have been met.

In the bilingual program, Cohen (1975) indicates that summative evaluation should be obtained over a period of years in each language, in academic achievement and in the students' attitudes. Cohen also mentions that all too often program evaluators assess students with yearly standardized tests in English without regard to measuring overall--cumulative--progress in both languages over a period of years.

The U.S. Commission for Civil Rights (1975) states that in a bilingual program the purpose of outcome (summative) evaluation is to determine the extent to which the bilingual-bicultural education program increased the educational progress of students in comparison with monolingual English instruction with or without ESL. Relative to bilingual programs, the present report has noted the inadequacy of standardized tests which do not use the language and culture of the target population. Without proper evaluation instruments and controls, however, it is difficult to compare progress made by students in bilingual programs with that made by students in monolingual programs. Some of the variables that would influence the results of a testing program are: (a) the students' entry-level of skills, (b) the students' language dominance, (c) the amount of time devoted to instruction in the home language and in English, (d) the nature of the evaluative instruments, (e) the attitude of the community and school toward the bilingual program and minority students, (f) the availability of quality instructional materials and (g) the preparation of the teachers in the area of bilingual education.

Although the Dissemination Center for Bilingual Bicultural Education (1975) has compiled an extensive annotated bibliography of evaluation instruments for use in bilingual programs, the truth of the matter is that there is a tremendous scarcity of hard data regarding the effectiveness of bilingual education programs. Proponents of this educational movement point to such things as improved self-concept, gains in the affective domain (Troike, 1974A) and increased school attendance. Opponents use underachievement as indicated on standardized tests as indicators of the failure of bilingual education. The reports of the Title VII projects vary in their findings and the data are usually not the result of rigorously controlled experiments. As a consequence, strong emotions--pro and con--have played a large role in the politics of bilingual education.

Recently the United States General Accounting Office (GAO) issued an important report to the Congress concerning the state of the art in bilingual education, *Bilingual Education: An Unmet Need* (1976). The report maintains that USOE has made little progress in identifying effective means of providing bilingual education instruction, training bilingual education teachers and developing suitable teaching materials. In reference to the first point, the report indicates that in 1971 USOE created a task force to determine whether or not bilingual education should change from a demonstration status to an educational service program. The committee recommended that effective strategies of bilingual education should be identified systematically. This recommendation was not carried out because of the cost of such a project and the inability of USOE to control the experiment in each local education agency (LEA).

Concerning point two, in March 1974, USOE had estimated that there were between 1.8 and 2.5 million children in need of bilingual education and that between 60,000 and 83,000 bilingual teachers would be needed (GAO, 1976). These figures were not accurate since they were based only on data from four states obtained from the 1970 census and on a study carried out by the Office for Civil Rights in 1972. Quantitatively, USOE has not been able to gather information concerning the skills and knowledge actually being provided by institutions of higher education (IHE) for future bilingual teachers. USOE has, however, specified that Title VII teachers meet the minimum qualifications of (GAO, 1976) bilingual capability, training and experience in teaching and using the native language of the target group as a medium of instruction, preparation and experience in ESL and awareness of the students' culture.

The GAO report states that the original Title VII legislation did not provide funds for scholarships or fellowships for individuals wishing to pursue a degree in bilingual education nor did it provide direct grants to IHE's. The 1974 Title VII amendments, however, have made this type of funding possible.

The third point of the report indicates the shortage of quality sequential materials, particularly in languages other than Spanish. LEA's, then, have been largely responsible for developing their own materials which are usually geared toward the specific needs of a given school district and adaptation by other LEA's has been difficult. The section of the present paper concerning materials indicates that Title VII funds are being used to develop materials in languages other than Spanish.

Longitudinal studies of student achievement are often made to measure student progress for a period of over one year. The GAO (1976) report reviewed student achievement in 16 projects and did a two-year longitudinal study:

> The analysis showed that 85, or 45 percent, of 191 English-dominant students and 67, or 33 percent, of 205 non-English dominant students made normal reading progress or better. In math, 73, or 57 percent, of 129 English-dominant students achieved at least normal progress. Thus, gains made by English-dominant students on the average were better than those of non-English-dominant students. Also, a comparison of the longitudinal results with the 1-year analysis shows that students generally did not achieve as high a rate of growth over the 2-year period as they did in 1 year. OE officials said that regression of this nature is common in all compensatory or remedial educational programs.

The report (GAO, 1976) goes on to state that two specific factors could have caused the foregoing results: (a) The dominant language of the limited English-speaking children might not have been used enough for classroom instruction. (b) There often seemed to be too many English-speaking children in the project classrooms, thereby diluting program services for the limited English-speaking children. While these reasons could very well affect the survey results, the report indicates that the analyses were done "...on English reading and English math tests given by the LEA as part of the regular school or Title VII testing program." It would seem, first of all, that this statement is contradictory to the explanations of the lower test scores by the non-English dominant students. If all-English tests were used, how can the insufficient use of the children's native language influence scores on these tests? Secondly, the tests were in English, even though some of the students were not dominant in this language. This procedure goes against the rationale for bilingual education--the use of the students' dominant language for instructional and evaluative purposes.

It seems that the GAO has pinpointed three particularly

acute areas of weakness in bilingual education. Although funds have been appropriated to create quality programs, the movement to teach children in two languages has had to face a number of obstacles like those identified by the GAO. It would appear unfair to try to compare the progress made in bilingual education since 1968 with that made in monolingual education which has a longer history, more experience and greater general support from the public.

On the other side of the coin, Dulay, Burt and Zappert (1976) have recently come forth with a summary of research findings graphically presented in a poster format. According to the authors, 28 research studies and 172 evaluation reports were excluded from the poster due to serious weaknesses in research design. Thus, the poster includes 66 findings from 9 research studies and three project evaluations. Although the number of actual studies is small, the authors conclude that:

> Contrary to widespread belief, the research conducted to date is not contradictory with regards to the effects of bilingualism and bilingual education on student performance. If one applies objective criteria for applicability and soundness of research design, most of the studies show a significant positive effect, or a nonsignificant effect, on student performance. Of the 66 findings reported here, only 1 (1%) was negative; 38 (58%) were positive, and 27 (41%) were neutral.

These positive findings are encouraging and should pave the way for more work in the area. Additionally, one can turn to other countries where bilingualism and bilingual education are a fact of life (Christian and Sharp, 1972):

> Bilingualism never seems to have impaired the intelligence of the social and intellectual elite of European countries where use of more than one major language is an important prerequisite for social position. Only where bilingualism is associated with a high degree of literacy in any two languages is it recognized as a form of achievement rather than limitation. Educational measures almost inevitably represent this cultural value.

STAFF DEVELOPMENT

University Programs

University teacher training programs in bilingual education and other related areas such as ethnic studies have increased dramatically since the passage of the 1968 bilingual legislation. Although there is little information available in terms of faculty qualifications, experience and courses of study, the increase in the number of programs is significant, since it points to interest in and demand for bilingual teaching personnel. Figures compiled from DACBE, *Teacher Education Programs for Bilingual Education in U.S. Colleges and Universities: 1974-75, 1975-76*, show this increase, particularly in terms of baccalaureate, master's and doctoral degree programs. For example, in 1974-75 there were 25 undergraduate programs in bilingual education in the nation, as compared to 96 in 1975-76; there were 43 master's programs in 1974-75 and 69 in 1975-76; in 1974-75 there were eight doctoral programs and 17 in 1975-76. DACBE's compilation also indicates other types of programs related to bilingual education, but these were somewhat difficult to compare, since the information from the sources was, at times, not too explicit and the various categories overlapped.

During fiscal year 1976, USOE, under Title VII, awarded a total of 700 fellowships for study at the master's and doctoral levels in the area of bilingual education. These fellowships were awarded to fellows enrolled in 38 universities and represent 12 different languages. These figures represent an increase over fiscal year 1975 when 480 fellowships were awarded to individuals enrolled in 30 universities. The purpose of the Title VII Bilingual Education Fellowship Program is to provide tuition, fees and stipends to individuals enrolled in an IHE which "...offers a program of study leading to a degree above the baccalaureate level in the field of training teachers for programs of bilingual education...(USOE, 1976)." The thrust of the fellowship program, therefore, is not to train bilingual classroom teachers, but to begin to meet the demand for teacher trainers who can staff IHE's. While programs of study vary among the participating IHE's, USOE primarily judges programs on their capability to teach courses in a language other than English, to teach culture, to select and use evaluative instruments for measuring performance of LESA children and to involve parents and community organizations in programs of bilingual education. It is hoped that the fellowship program will help to alleviate the present shortage of teacher trainers and will assist in institutionalizing bilingual education programs in IHE's throughout the country.

A vital dimension of university programs is training for bilingual classroom teachers. Before the 1974 Title VII amendments, the majority of training activities were provided through in-service programs, utilizing at times consultants from colleges and universities. Although USOE is not a regulatory agency, it sets general standards for bilingual education teacher training programs through its funding programs. State education agency certification standards for a bilingual credential, on the other hand, vary considerably. In an attempt to provide leadership in bilingual education teacher training, the Center for Applied Linguistics (CAL) produced its *Guidelines for the Preparation and Certification of Teachers of Bilingual/Bicultural Education* (1974). The various categories are those that the writing committee felt were indispensable for the bilingual education teacher. These categories are, in turn, expressed or broken down into competencies which the "ideal" bilingual education teacher should demonstrate: Ideal in that it would be a rare individual who could be expected to perform all the identified competencies. They do, however, identify important areas of the bilingual program which the teacher should strive to attain.

Palmer (1975), a proponent of competency-based teacher education (CBTE) in bilingual education, states that "CBTE will not guarantee that all graduates of the program will be excellent teachers. It will...provide a just, equitable and systematic method of training teachers in a fast-changing field that needs exceptional personnel." Palmer's competency categories are somewhat similar to those proposed by CAL. They include working with children and with parents, cultural interaction, diagnosis and prescription, communication skills in the native language, mathematics, social studies, science, health and physical education, art, music, creativity and personal and professional development.

A concern in CBTE is determining levels of competency, that is, establishing criteria and strategies by which to assess an individual's ability to perform a given skill or to apply a theory to a practical situation. With this in mind, The University of Texas at Austin (UT Austin) subcontracted under Title VII with CAL (1976) to develop criterion measures and evaluative instruments for the following competencies listed in the *Guidelines*:

Area:	*Personal Qualities*
Competency:	A thorough knowledge of and proficiency in the child's home language and the ability to teach content through it; an understanding of the nature of the language the child brings with him and the ability to utilize it as a positive tool in his teaching.
Area:	*Language Proficiency*
Competency:	Carry out instruction in all areas of the curriculum using a standard variety of both languages.
Area:	*Linguistics*
Competency:	Identify and understand structural differences between the child's first and

second languages, recognizing areas of potential interference and positive transfer.

Area: *Culture*
Competency: Understand, appreciate and incorporate into activities, materials and other aspects of the instructional environment: (a) The culture and history of the group's ancestry. (b) Contributions of group to history and culture of the United States. (c) Contemporary life style(s) of the group.

Area: *Instructional Methods*
Competency: Organize, plan, and teach specific lessons in the required curriculum areas, using the appropriate terminology in the learner's language(s) and observing the local district curriculum guidelines. Basic elements and methodologies best suited to the teaching of reading and language arts, mathematics, social studies and science as a minimum, must be identified and applied in the learner's language(s)....Utilize effective classroom management techniques, for optimal learning in specific situations.

These measures were pilot-tested with a group of experienced bilingual teachers and are being further refined during the 1976-77 academic year. At the same time UT Austin will continue to develop additional measures for other competencies identified in the *Guidelines*. It is felt that these measures will serve as a model for other bilingual teacher training programs to do additional work in CBTE.

The emphasis of university programs has been the training of teachers and teacher trainers and this is shown in the information provided by the 1974-75 and 1975-76 editions of DACBE publications on teacher education which did not identify any university programs that offered administrative degrees or other credentials in bilingual education. If this is the case, it would seem that colleges and universities should now begin expanding their programs to encompass the area of bilingual program administration. To ensure the growth and strengthening of bilingual education, knowledgeable and qualified bilingual education administrators, such as coordinators, principals, supervisors and superintendents, are an absolute necessity.

In-service Education

Title VII provides funds to LEA's to support ongoing in-service activities for teachers. LEA's may request funds to implement in-service programs through the use of consultants or they may request funds to provide in-service training in the form of university programs--usually leading toward an advanced degree.

Locally sponsored in-service activities vary greatly in scope and topics. An ERIC search of LEA in-service programs revealed 26 topics. The topics are presented in Table 5 on page 53.

It can be noted that many of the topics presented in the table are similar to those identified by CAL and by Palmer. The CAL *Guidelines* constitute a well developed list of categories and competencies which LEA's can use as a model to develop ongoing in-service programs for bilingual education teachers. The ERIC search did not reveal the extent to which the target languages of the programs were used in the in-service sessions. It would be safe to assume, however, that the majority of activities were carried out in English. Language development for teachers in the non-English languages of bilingual programs is an area of concern, since many teachers have had limited formal training in these languages, despite their being native speakers (Blanco, 1975). One can only hope that, as bilingual education programs grow, in-service programs will use ever-increasing amounts of the target languages in the activities for teachers. The in-service programs will, thus, be practicing what they recommend for the children's curriculum: Language development in the target language of the bilingual program.

ISSUES CRITICAL TO THE FUTURE OF BILINGUAL EDUCATION

Attitudes Toward Bilingual Education

The funding which bilingual education has received can be viewed as support for this educational movement. There is much interest in bilingual education at the present time as indicated by the ever-increasing programs at the local, state and federal levels, and support has also been forthcoming from other educational fields, such as mathematics and social studies. Another segment which has rallied to the aid of bilingual education is the community. Martin (1975) reports that most Amerindian groups welcome the inclusion of native languages in the curriculum, although there is still some resistance stemming from the notion that the English language and English speaking teachers are superior. Gutiérrez (1972) also noted that parents in her New Mexico study showed a positive attitude toward bilingual education, and underscored the importance of parental support for the

Table 5

Topics Presented in In-Service Programs

(McBride, 1974)

	ED 065 212	ED 065 212 (Jefferson)	ED 065 212 (Empire Gardens)	ED 057 973	ED 065 221	ED 071 795	ED 081 549	ED 041 066	ED 064 024	ED 067 197	ED 066 983
Encounter Group			x								
Human Relations Training								x			
Reading: Skills	x	x							x		x
Reading: Diagnosis	x	x			x		x	x			x
Oral Language Development	x	x			x						
Relate Art, Music, Linguistics or Use Any of These	x				x				x		
Contrastive Analysis of Languages					x						x
Teaching Spanish to Spanish Speakers					x						
ESL or Second Language Learning					x	x				xx	
Rationale for Bilingual Program						x	x		x	x	x
Evaluation Design of Program					x	x				x	
Information on Materials		x		x				x			x
Individualized Instruction				x			x				
Behavior Modification/Positive Reinforcement				x					x	x	
Culture				x	x		x	x		x	
Classroom Arrangement				x				x			
Teaching Socialization Skills				x					x		
Involving Parents					x						
Interaction Analysis					x						
Writing Behavioral Objectives		x			x						
Lesson Planning								x			
Testing							x		x	x	
Cognitive & Intellectual Development									x		
Use of Audio-Visual Equipment							x			x	
Roles of Teachers and Staff									x	x	
Community Resources										x	
Curriculum Development							x	x	x	x	

success of the bilingual program. In another survey (Flores Macías, 1973), parents indicated very favorable support for bilingual preschool education programs. Greene and Zirkel (1973) reported that bilingual parents were found to have a more positive attitude about bilingualism than their monolingual counterparts. Lest we paint an overly positive picture of attitudes toward the use of languages other than English in American education, it is necessary to examine some of the contrary positions.

Albert Shanker (1974) of the United Federation of Teachers made the following statement aimed at bilingual education programs:

> While the need for the child to feel comfortable and to be able to communicate is clear, it is also clear that what these children need is intensive instruction in English so that they may as soon as possible function with other children in regular school programs....The American taxpayer, while recognizing the existence of cultural diversity, still wants the schools to be the basis of an American melting pot.

This statement, designed to appeal to the uninformed and to educators who feel their livelihood threatened by the bilingual education movement, does not mention that the learning of English is one of the basic goals of U.S. bilingual education.

More recently, a *Long Island Press* columnist also made strong statements against the teaching of languages other than English (Cuneo, 1975):

> If the parents of these children are too lazy or too ignorant to learn the American language, they ought not to be voting citizens....The emphasis, therefore, should be upon teaching their children the American language to overcome the disadvantage of their parents. The object of American schooling is to teach them to think as Americans, not to continue the customs of a different culture.

This columnist goes on to say that these [minority] children are already learning the "nasty" lesson of not having acquired the American language because "...third-rate politicians are bent on acquiring the votes of their parents." These are only two examples of opposition to the bilingual education movement; there are other individuals over the nation who are speaking out against it and emphasizing its failure to produce quality education. Jaramillo (1973) exhorts bilingual educators to "...support and expand good bicultural programs with or without federal funds...[and]...to eradicate poor programs.... We cannot, we must not, give these critics food for thought. We must produce excellent programs only." Not only must we produce excellent programs, but we must continuously inform the public of our successes through the news media, parent-teacher groups and civic organizations. Public support is vital to the continuation of bilingual education.

Another dimension of attitudes toward bilingual education lies within the ranks of bilingual educators. A great deal of parochialism still exists within the field. Presumably, bilingual educators are striving to achieve common goals. Yet, we see little effort to engage in serious educational exchange programs whereby the Southwest, for example, could benefit by hiring Puerto Ricans or the Northeast could strengthen its concept of the Hispanic world by recruiting Mexican American teachers. Although bilingual education should present a united front, the internal division even within a particular language group will eventually prove to be detrimental to the very goals toward which the profession is striving: Maintenance bilingual education for LESA and for mainstream children.

Federal Funding

The impact of Title VII funds on bilingual education has yet to make the favorable impression which the authors of the Bilingual Education Act had hoped. The resistance previously indicated and the problems hindering more visible progress have reflected poorly on the movement. It is significant, however, that many of the problem areas--lack of qualified teaching personnel, quality instructional materials and good curriculum models for program implementation--are just now being addressed by the Title VII amendments of 1974. Although teachers within the ranks of bilingual education have often become discouraged by the many obstacles, the future in terms of the above three elements is somewhat brighter.

The funding made available under the National Defense Education Act (NDEA) of 1958 was "seed money" designed to assist schools and colleges to upgrade and institutionalize their instructional programs. The intent of NDEA was for local and state education agencies to eventually assume fiscal and program responsibilities. The same intent is present in the Title VII legislation. There are indications that federal support for bilingual education will increase. Molina (1977) states that USOE will ask Congress for increased funding to allow for such critical areas as teacher training, research and provisions to include mainstream students in bilingual education programs. In spite of this possibility, however, schools cannot and should not rely exclusively on federal funds for bilingual education program implementation. Programs may receive funding for only a specified period of time and funding approval may often cease for one of several reasons: (a) The "seed money" has had an impact on a local program and USOE officials feel that the money would be better utilized in another LEA. (b) The local program receives an unfavorable evaluation and is no longer considered a good investment of federal funds. (c) The appropriation of funds is usually insufficient to allow 100 percent approval of all LEA project proposals. Thus, while total federal funding approved by the Congress may continue to increase, it would be unrealistic to expect total funding for every local bilingual education program in the country.

LEA's, state boards of education and state legislatures must include bilingual education funding as an integral part of their public school financial plans. The Council of Chief State School Officers has gone on record as supporting cultural pluralism (Council of Chief State School Officers, 1977), and this action must be capitalized on to ensure that state boards of education incorporate bilingual education into the curriculum for general education. If the profession has established high standards for its bilingual programs and the results of the programs are widely disseminated, school boards and the general public will be more inclined not only to accept bilingual education, but also to provide funding for them, once federal monies are withdrawn.

Likewise colleges and universities will have to assume the financial responsibility for training bilingual education teachers and teacher trainers. Although the number of IHE's with bilingual bicultural programs has increased greatly with the availability of federal funds, some IHE bilingual programs predate the Title VII 1974 amendments which provided them with direct grants.

Training of Personnel

With the present state and federal efforts in teacher training, the demand for qualified bilingual personnel will be somewhat alleviated. Despite federal assistance to IHE's and the state efforts in teacher preparation, however, this writer is cautious in being overly optimistic about the training of sufficient numbers of personnel necessary to make a serious impact on bilingual education programs in the near future. Although there is no information presently available concerning the national need for bilingual education teachers, the figure must be large, since Texas alone needed 5,000 bilingual education teachers for 1976-77 (Cruz-Aedo, 1976).

The training of teachers and teacher aides has advanced from a purely in-service activity to one sponsored by IHE's, which may lead to a degree, certification or both. The Title VII Fellowship Program is helping to prepare teacher trainers and the next generation of bilingual teachers will, undoubtedly, be better trained than those in the past. However, IHE's are faced with one of the very same problems that many local schools are trying to cope with: The tremendous scarcity of personnel proficient in languages other than English.

To be sure, IHE's should practice what they preach and should be in a position to conduct courses either bilingually or completely in the non-English language, but university personnel with this linguistic capability are still very rare. Local schools look to the colleges and universities to train their teachers. This presumes that the IHE's have the necessary personnel themselves. They do not at this time.

IHE's with bilingual personnel training programs need that rare individual who has a pedagogical background, has academic training in two languages and usually has a doctorate in hand. The only solution to the problem is genuine cooperation among the various disciplines and departments that comprise bilingual education--both in the professional field of education and in other areas, such as the humanities, science, etc. It is also a question of the IHE administration not being too hasty in abolishing positions earmarked for bilingual personnel simply because such individuals are not readily available.

Another need for bilingual education personnel lies within the ranks of administration. This paper has indicated the central role of various administrators to the success of bilingual education programs. IHE's must now begin to think seriously about developing training programs and certification programs for bilingual education administrators. This should either take the form of a specialist in bilingual education administration or should consist of a supporting field for any administrative credential or degree from IHE's located in states with large numbers of bilingual education programs. Indubitably, administrative support is essential to the success of bilingual education programs.

Maintenance and Transitional Bilingual Education

Federal and state legislation dictates transitional bilingual education. While advocates of bilingual education can rationalize the transitional model on the grounds that "it gets our foot in the door," one cannot but wonder about the psychological damage and educational waste occasioned by this approach. The child quickly comes to understand that phasing out his home language must mean that it is inferior or that something is wrong with it. Educationally the nation squanders a great resource by not developing languages other than English spoken natively in America. To be sure, initiating programs using a transitional or compensatory model is a beginning, but it should be just that--a beginning. We cannot stand by complacently accepting tokenism, but must demand recognition of one of our greatest educational opportunities. If bilingual education in the United States is to survive, it must move quickly into a language maintenance model. Even more, it must cease to be a program for "disadvantaged" minorities and incorporate the mainstream society. The hearings held before the National Advisory Council on Bilingual Education in Austin in January 1977 and in New Orleans in April 1977 (Molina, 1976,1977) clearly underscore and endorse the need for maintenance bilingual education. Fishman (1976) strongly advocates a form of bilingual education which is even more widespread internationally than the language maintenance model. He calls it enrichment bilingual education and points out that this is the kind of education opted for by the elites in 3,000 years of recorded world history. This is the type of bilingual education needed in the United States, the type which would include all pupils--not just minorities--and thus be an integral part of general education.

Research

One of the most important areas concerning the future of bilingual education is research. As was previously indicated, longitudinal studies on bilingual education are almost nonexistent. At the present time, bilingual education is heavily supported by federal funding. Taxpayers not only look closely at the money spent on education in general, but particularly at programs they consider controversial, unnecessary or undesirable. While we can point to the success of bilingual schooling abroad, the truth of the matter is that American taxpayers want to see successful educational programs in their own schools. In the final analysis, bilingual education will have to depend on local and state support if it is to become an integral part of general education. The level of future state and local financial support, however, will depend largely on the reputation of past programs. If they have been successful and the public is thereby convinced that bilingual education is not a frill or just a compensatory program for "disadvantaged" minorities but an indispensable part of the regular educational program, then the chances for continued support will be far greater.

What are the research needs in bilingual education today? What has been done? What remains to be done? In terms of needs, Troike (1974B) identified 12 research priorities in bilingual education and they include such topics as: (a) Sociolinguistic research on regional and social variations in the use of Spanish and English by Spanish speaking communities in the United States, especially in the Southwest. (b) Research on the effect of different instructional methods with different linguistic and cultural groups, and with different age groups. (c) Research on the effect of teacher attitudes on student achievement, the effect of bilingual teaching on student self-concept and the effect of linguistically and anthropologically oriented teacher training on teacher behavior and student achievement. (d) Research on the effect of bilingual education programs on school-community relations, and of community attitudes on school and language achievement. (e) Research on problems of transfer from native language reading to reading in English.

The Multicultural/Bilingual Division of the National Institute of Education (1976) has identified four general areas in which it will support research and development:

> Policy studies to provide information to educational policy makers necessary for making decisions on bilingual programs;
>
> Linguistic research to increase the knowledge base relative to native and second language acquisition in order to enhance the effectiveness of bilingual education for persons of limited English speaking ability;
>
> Assessment procedures to develop new methods and instruments for identifying students in need of bilingual education and for assessing the educational progress of bilingual students;
>
> Teaching and curriculum development to improve the instructional processes utilized in bilingual/multicultural programs at the elementary and secondary levels.

In its continued efforts to promote quality research in the area of bilingual education, NIE in March 1977 sponsored a conference designed "to explore strategies for coordinating and supporting the dissertation research work of the ESEA Title VII doctoral fellows (Vázquez and Miller, 1977)." The conference underscored the need to promote quality research and to avoid duplication of efforts among the bilingual education doctoral students. USOE will propose changes in the Title VII legislation to include funds for research in bilingual education (Molina, 1977).

Since research is such a crucial component of the continuation of bilingual education at this time, it is indeed sad that this educational concept not be given a fair chance to prove its worth in most of the research now being done. According to a recent news release from HEW (1977), the Office of Education reported interim findings of a national evaluation of bilingual education, conducted by the American Institutes for Research (1977), which indicate that the program is producing mixed results. According to the news release, the evaluation involved 38 Spanish-English projects in 11 states in their fourth and fifth year of Title VII funding. Students in grades six-seven (approximately 5,300 Title VII students and some 2,400 students of similar background not enrolled in the program) were tested in fall of 1975 and in spring of 1976. According to the release, major findings of the study are:

> Only one-third of the students enrolled in bilingual education classrooms were of limited English speaking ability.
>
> During a 5½ month period Title VII Hispanic students made smaller progress in English language proficiency than their non-program counterparts, but showed greater gains in mathematics.
>
> 86% of the Title VII project directors reported that Spanish dominant students often remain in bilingual classrooms after they are able to function in English.

The Center for Applied Linguistics (CAL) has prepared a response to the AIR study (1977) and charges that, in general, the study treats all bilingual education programs alike without regard to differences. According to CAL the major drawbacks of the AIR study are: (a) weakness of pre- and post-test design over a five month period; (b) inappropriate use of gain scores to assess effects of experimental treatments; (c) unreliability of teacher assessment of students' language ability; (d) inappropriate use of the CTBS [California Test of Basic Skills] to assess English reading ability with limited English and monolingual Spanish speakers, possibly invalidating the results; (e) lack of adequate teacher training and curriculum during the first five years of Title VII funding; (f) distortion of information which defeats the intended purpose of the report, i.e. to provide information for policy makers and (g) aggregation of students who have received a variety of educational treatments funded by Title VII and whose language ability ranges from monolingual English to bilingual to monolingual Spanish conceals the potential effect of bilingual education. As indicated earlier, most of the research studies have been rejected because of inherent weaknesses in the research design (Dulay, Burt and Zappert, 1976), such as no control for subjects' socio-economic status, no control for initial language proficiency, no baseline comparison data or control group, inadequate sample, excessive attrition rate, significant differences in teacher qualifications for control and experimental groups and insufficient data and/or statistics reported.

A considerable amount of research on language, bilingualism and bilingual education has been conducted as a result of the Language Research Project of The University of

Texas at Austin (Horn, 1976). The research consists primarily of dissertations beginning in 1964.

To be sure, not a great deal of quality research has been conducted in the field of bilingual education. It is only fair, therefore, that findings be presented as objectively as possible and that variables be accounted for, and not merely ignored as has been the case in most instances up to now. With criticisms such as those reported here, it is not possible to lend credence to the negative reports concerning bilingual education. It is not until serious, well-designed studies are conducted that we can obtain a true picture of the effects of bilingual education.

Despite the dismal state of the art in research in the area of bilingual education, Dulay, Burt and Zappert (1976) were able to report positive findings on those studies and project evaluations that met the strict criteria which they established. They concluded that "...the research conducted to date strongly supports the use of the child's first learned, dominant, and/or home language as a medium of instruction in U.S. schools."

CONCLUSION

The melting pot philosophy, though still prevalent in the minds of many American citizens, is being challenged. What we have today is a legacy of the turbulent Sixties: It is still a time of questioning, of search for identity--but this quest is somewhat less intense; it is less emotional and more objective. The civil rights movement led the struggle for equal rights. Though we as a nation have come a long way in this quest, much remains to be done. I have attempted to show that America is a culturally and linguistically pluralistic society whether mainstream society is willing to recognize it or not. There is nothing inherently wrong with this diversity. This diversity, whether it is based on lifestyle, culture or language, must be seen as a strength--as an affirmation that we are secure in our self-identity as citizens of this country and in the belief of the very tenets on which the nation was founded.

There is nothing within the philosophy of bilingual education that diminishes the reality that English is the official language of the United States. There is nothing in the philosophy of bilingual education to support the fear that it encourages political, linguistic or cultural fragmentation of the nation. There is nothing to support the notion that linguistic and cultural diversity is categorically linked with political alienation. Bilingual education reaffirms all these concepts.

Viewing diversity as a strength, most bilingual education practitioners support maintenance as opposed to transitional education programs. The maintenance concept encourages the intellectual development of individuals who function in two cultures and who are fully competent in two languages: They understand, speak, read and write English and another language. This philosophy is different from the transitional model where the individual is quickly moved into English at the expense of the other language and culture. The transitional model is contradictory to the educational philosophy of our nation, which advances the needs of individuals and the satisfaction of their human wants. To date, bilingual education has been viewed as a program for "disadvantaged" students. From this point of view bilingualism is seen as a deficiency rather than a strength as in other parts of the world where it is the uneducated person who is monolingual.

It is important for critics who claim that bilingual education and bilingualism are harmful to realize that there is little in terms of serious, well-designed and carefully controlled research that upholds this viewpoint. What little, good research is available indicates that bilingual education is either beneficial in terms of scholastic achievement or that it is neutral--in which case the individual has the added advantage of coming out of the experience as one who has been exposed to two languages. Much more serious research in bilingual education needs to be done to improve the quality of the curriculum, instructional procedures and teaching materials for children with limited English speaking skill. Much work also needs to be done to explore ways of including children from the mainstream society into bilingual education programs.

It is not until individuals from all segments of American society are given the opportunity of participating in bilingual and multicultural experiences that the U.S. will prove its mettle, its ability to recognize individual freedom. Individuality, and thereby diversity, is a source of strength and a basic human right which transcends political boundaries. In direct opposition to Israel Zangwill's call for unity through amalgamation in the melting pot, cultural and linguistic pluralism responds to an earlier call for unity:

I swear I begin to see the meaning of these things,
It is not the earth, it is not America who is so great,
It is I who am great or to be great, it is You up there, or
any one,
It is to walk rapidly through civilizations, governments,
theories,
Through poems, pageants, shows, to form individuals.

Underneath all, individuals,
I swear nothing is good to me now that ignores individuals,
The American compact is altogether with individuals,
The only government is that which makes minute of individuals,
The whole theory of the universe is directed unerringly to
one single individual--namely to You.--Walt Whitman

Acknowledgments

I would like to express my appreciation to the following for their assistance and cooperation in the preparation of this paper: Nona Blanchard, The University of Texas at Austin; Joanna Chambers, Dissemination and Assessment Center, Austin, Texas; Josefina Rodríguez-Gibbs, The University of Texas at Austin; Lupe Gómez, The University of Texas at Austin. I would especially like to express my sincere thanks and appreciation to Bobby LaBouve, Texas Education Agency, for his encouragement and invaluable assistance in critiquing and editing this manuscript.

Appendix A

Language Dominance Tests and Language Proficiency Tests

DOMINANCE TESTS

Bilingual Syntax Measure

Harcourt-Brace-Jovanovich
757 Third Avenue
New York, NY 10017

Ambiguous Verbal Stimulus Test and Flexibility Test to Measure Language Dominance

G.D. Keller
Department of Romance Languages
City College of New York
New York, NY 10031

Comprehension of Oral Language (Inter-American Series)

Guidance Testing Associates of St. Mary's University
One Camino Santa Maria
San Antonio, TX 78284

Home Bilingual Usage Estimate

R.V. Skoczylas
7649 Santa Inez Court
Gilroy, CA 95020

Spolsky Spanish-English Language Dominance Assessment

B. Spolsky
University of New Mexico
1805 Roma, NE
Albuquerque, NM 87131

Tests of Basic Language Competence in English and Spanish

E.J. Cervenka
617 West End Avenue, Suite 9-A
New York, NY 10024

James Language Dominance Test

Learning Concepts, Speech Division
2501 North Lamar
Austin, TX 78705

S/ELPS (Spanish/English Language Performance Sample)

Joyce Evans
Southwest Educational Development Laboratory
211 East Seventh Street
Austin, TX 78701

TOLD Tests of Language Dominance

Southwest Research Associates
PO Box 4092
Albuquerque, NM 87106

Language Dominance Index Form

California State Department of Educatio
State Education Building
721 Capitol Mall
Sacramento, CA 95814

Marysville Test of Language Dominance

Eleanor Thonis
Marysville Reading-Learning Center
11th Avenue and Powerline Road
Olivehurst, CA 95961

Bilingual Dominance Scale

Project BEST, New York City Board of Education
110 Livingston Street, Rm. 601-C
Brooklyn, NY 11201

PROFICIENCY TESTS

Basic Inventory of Natural Language (BINL)

Chess and Associates, Inc.
PO Box 833
San Bernardino, CA 92401

Primary Acquisition of Language (PAL) Oral Language Dominance Measure English/Spanish

Alicia Trevino
Coordinator of Elementary Education
6531 Boeing Drive
El Paso, TX 79925

Language Facility Test

J.T. Dailey
Allington Corporation
801 North Pitt Street
Alexandria, VA 22314

OLÉ (Oral Language Evaluation) English/Spanish

N.J. Silvaroli
D.A. Lewis Associates
7801 Old Branch Avenue, Suite 201
Clinton, MD 20735

s Amigos Verbal Language Scale
glish/Spanish

Donald E. Critchlow, Author
Academic Therapy Publications
1539 Fourth Street
San Rafael, CA 94901

al Language Proficiency Test

Moreno Education Company
7050 Belle Glade Lane
San Diego, CA 92119

CEL (Test of Oral English Production)

Southwestern Cooperative Education
Laboratory, Inc.
229 Truman, NE
Albuquerque, NM 87108

T-SEA-CAL (Matluck/Mace-Matluck)

Center for Applied Linguistics
815 Fourth Avenue North
Seattle, WA 98109

loria and David-Oral Bilingual Test
nglish

Language Arts, Inc.
Mrs. Dennis Welch
3102 Maywood Avenue
Austin, TX 78703

TACL (Screening Test for Auditory
omprehension of Language)
ACL (Test for Auditory Comprehension of
anguage)

Learning Concepts, Speech Division
2501 North Lamar
Austin, TX 78705

he Auditory Pointing Test (English)

Academic Therapy Publications
1539 Fourth Street
San Rafael, CA 94901

eabody Picture Vocabulary Test English/
Spanish

American Guidance Service, Inc.
Publishers' Building
Circle Pines, MN 55014

APELL (Assessment Program of Early
Learning Levels)

Edcodyne Corporation
One City Boulevard West, Suite 935
Orange, CA 92668

Auditory Discrimination Test (ADT)

Language Research Associates
175 East Delaware Place
Chicago, IL 60611

Comprehensive English Language Test (CELT)

F. Perkins
McGraw-Hill International Book Company
1221 Avenue of the Americas
New York, NY 10020

Diagnostic Test for Students of English
as a Second Language

F. Perkins
McGraw-Hill International Book Company
1221 Avenue of the Americas
New York, NY 10020

Hebrew Language Tests (Hebrew)

National Testing Bureau
American Association for Jewish Education
114 Fifth Avenue
New York, NY 10011

Ilyin Oral Interview

D. Ilyin
Newbury House Publishers
68 Middle Road
Rowley, MA 01969

Structured Response Test (SRT) and
Conceptual Oral Language Test (COLT)

Modern Language Association
Publications Center
62 Fifth Avenue
New York, NY 10011

MLA-Cooperative Foreign Language Tests

Educational Testing Service
Box 999
Princeton, NJ 08540

Pimsleur Modern Foreign Language Pro-
ficiency Tests

Harcourt-Brace-Jovanovich, Inc.
757 Third Avenue
New York, NY 10017

Pruebas de Puerto Rico

Oficina de Evaluación
Departamento de Instrucción Pública
Hato Rey, Estado Libre Asociado de
Puerto Rico

English Phonemic Unit Production Test and
Spanish Phonemic Unit Production Test

R.V. Skoczylas
8459 Gary Street
Gilroy, CA 95020

Tests of Basic Language Competence in
English and Spanish (TBLC)

E.J. Cervenka
617 West End Avenue, Suite 9-A
New York, NY 10024

ZIP Test (Language Facility Section)

California State Department of Education
721 Capitol Mall
Sacramento, CA 95814

Foreign Service Institute Oral Proficiency Interview

Department of State
Foreign Service Institute
Washington, DC 20520

Ott Test of Oral Language English and Spanish

Southwest Education Development Laboratory
211 East Seventh Street
Austin, TX 78701

Peace Corps Oral Proficiency Battery

Educational Testing Service
Princeton, NJ 08540

Test of English as a Second Language (TOEFL)

Educational Testing Service
Princeton, NJ 08540

Linguistic Capacity Index (English)

Southwest Educational Development Laboratory
211 East Seventh Street
Austin, TX 78701

Michigan Oral Language Test

Michigan Department of Education
Evaluation Director, Michigan Migrant Primary Interdisciplinary Project
3800 Packard Road
Ann Arbor, MI 48104

Perfil

Carol Perkins
Region XIII Education Service Center
6504 Tracor Lane
Austin, TX 78721

Spanish Test of Oral Proficiency

Bay Area Bilingual Education League Media Center
1033 Heinz Street
Berkeley, CA 94710

Tucson Public Schools Language Assessmen

Tucson School District 1
1010 East 10th Street
Tucson, AZ 85719

Viewpoints

viewpoint: Jose A. Cardenas

Budgeting for Bilingual Education

The Intercultural Development Research Association (IDRA) is a non-profit Texas corporation dedicated to the concept of equal education opportunity. Among the many activities conducted by the organization is the affording of equitable and adequate instructional programs to all children by a system of financing state education which eliminates the tremendous disparities currently existing between the tax rich and the tax poor school districts in the state. Of equal importance in the organization's work is the development and implementation of alternative education programs which afford to each child--regardless of racial, ethnic or sex characteristics--a unique instructional program carefully developed according to specifications based on the personal and unique characteristics of each individual child. Much of the work of the organization is devoted to research, development and implementation of bilingual education programs--primarily for children of limited English speaking ability.

It was inevitable that our interest in the adequate financing of schools and our interest in bilingual education programs interphase in a special project funded by the U.S. Office of Education to determine the cost of an adequate bilingual education program. This project was conducted during the 1975-76 school year, and was terminated in the summer of 1976.

BILINGUAL COST ANALYSIS PROJECT

The project, directed by former State Senator Joe J. Bernal of San Antonio, and assisted by William L. Kean, was a unique adventure into no man's land since each project activity consisted of a venture into virgin territory--areas in which no educators, educational researchers or research institutions had previously explored.

It seems unbelievable that during the past decade when federal appropriations for bilingual education grew from $5 million to almost $100 million, when more than 30 state legislatures made legislative provisions for bilingual education and when at least 11 state legislatures had appropriated funds for the implementation of bilingual education programs, that nobody had addressed the question of "How much does it cost to provide an adequate program in bilingual education?"

An early analysis of the research in the funding of bilingual education programs failed to turn up a single activity directed toward this purpose. Recommendations made to legislative groups were either based on political considerations or, more commonly, on cost analyses of other programs for atypical children. Both Texas and Florida had performed cost analyses for compensatory education programs, and using the erroneous assumption that bilingual education is a type of compensatory education, made legislative recommendations for funding at the same level already determined appropriate for compensatory education.

Best Practice Methodology

Most studies related to educational costs conducted in the past have been based on a "light house" or "best practice" methodology. The rationale utilized in this methodology is that the cost of an education program can be determined by the identification of an exemplary program and an analysis of funds currently being expended in such a program. The utilization of such a "best practice" methodology inevitably produces two serious problems.

First, the identification of a "best practice" school district is a highly subjective activity and often reflects the strength of public relations departments in competing school districts as well as staff and district popularity, rather than an objective determination of program efficiency and effectiveness. The second problem which manifests itself in a state like Texas is that general and average expenditures for education are consistently below national averages. Determining the cost of an adequate program in a state which normally ranks 40th in state per pupil expenditures may identify "best practices" which, through financial constraints, are inadquate to begin with. The resulting cost analysis usually reflects the below average state expenditures.

IDRA's cost analysis of bilingual education encountered a third problem. Bilingual education programs are such a recent innovation that essential elements (staff preparation, materials development and organization) are in such a state of evolution, no program can currently be identified as an exemplary program reflecting the rationale, preparation and practices deemed essential for an adequate bilingual education program. This finding does not imply that there are no "good" bilingual programs in Texas. It only reflects that even the best programs have a long way to go in terms of subject matter coverage, curriculum materials and staffing before they can be classified as an adequate representation of a theoretically sound bilingual education program.

Project Methodology

In order to by-pass the three problems listed above, the Cost Analysis Project impaneled a group of bilingual education experts consisting of practitioners in the field and representatives of institutions of higher education and state and national education agencies. This panel of experts proceeded to develop a hypothetical, minimally adequate bilingual education program, determined the components of such a hypothetical program, identified the personnel and material services needed for implementation of the program and analyzed the cost of providing such support. In every case, the cost of support services was determined on the basis of school district expenditures in bilingual or monolingual programs, or direct communications with the supplier.

The analysis of bilingual education costs was further complicated by the existence of two concepts which tend to produce distorted and invalid figures. The first concept was the provision of funds for the education of minority or disadvantaged children on a categorized basis in order to compensate for inadequacies in a state system of school finance. In such instances, children of limited English speaking ability may serve as a proxy for distribution of funds in order to reduce disparities in the state system.

An example of this concept is the state of New Mexico in which school districts enrolling children of limited English speaking ability receive a bilingual education add-on amounting to 50 percent of the district expenditure per pupil. These "bilingual education" funds are made available to each school district regardless of whether it implements a bilingual education program or not, let alone the type, extent and quality of bilingual education programs to be implemented.

Though Texas does not present such a clear case of a proxy, it is evident that some compensatory education, special education and bilingual education funding serves as a proxy for low tax wealth school districts.

A much more complicated problem in analyzing expenditures in bilingual education is the tendency for innovative programs to serve as catalysts for improvements in the general education program. New programs--particularly federally funded programs--seem to demand a liberal sprinkling of gadgets and gimmicks far above what school districts can afford or do supply for the regular programs. It is not uncommon to discover school situations in which the "new federal program" provides motion picture and slide projectors, overhead transparencies, tape recorders and duplicating equipment which are unknown in traditional programs.

Though there is nothing wrong with bilingual education serving as a catalyst for the upgrading of the entire school program, it is highly questionable whether the cost of such upgrading should be attributed to the cost of bilingual education. The analysis of bilingual education costs should serve as an estimate of the cost of extending a monolingual program through bilingual offerings, but should not include bilingual education support for the monolingual program itself. Therefore, it was determined early in the study that costs would be analyzed for a minimally adequate bilingual education program, in most cases comparable to the monolingual offerings, and if indirect benefits are accrued to regular instructional programs, it would be a desirable spin-off of the bilingual program, but not at its expense.

Incidental to the conducting of this study, project staff, as well as panel experts providing direction for the study, were continuously appalled by the absence of information concerning school district expenditures and bilingual education support. With very limited exceptions, school districts generally had little information, let alone acceptable documentation or justification for the expenditure of funds in programmatic activities. It was evident in this project that there is a need for state and local accountability procedures which present an adequate picture of the expenditure of public money, the efficiency of school systems utilizing the funds and the effectiveness of such expenditures in terms of improved pupil outcomes.

FINDINGS

Variables Which Influence the Cost

It was assumed at the beginning of the project that the cost of a bilingual education program would be dependent on a variety of characteristics associated with that program. The first of these hypotheses identified four variables which influence the cost of a bilingual education program.

Grade Level. In general, the cost of a bilingual education program diminishes at each level through the fifth grade. As in regular monolingual instructional programs, kindergarten bilingual education programs were found to be the most expensive, followed by the first grade, second grade, etc. up to the fifth grade level. The main reason for the influence of this variable is the nature of the Texas School Foundation Program which allocates a much smaller pupil to teacher ratio at the lower grades than at the intermediate levels.

Year of Implementation. Start-up costs the first year that a bilingual education program is implemented at any grade level produces a significantly higher cost for the bilingual education program the first year than in subsequent years. The cost of operation further diminishes in the third and fourth years though the amount of reduction is rather minimal.

Prior Staffing Patterns. The largest dependent variable in determining the cost of a bilingual education program proved to be the characteristics of instructional staff including teachers, supervisors and administrators prior to the implementation of the bilingual education program. School districts which had a plentiful supply of bilingual personnel tended to have an easy time of implementing a bilingual education program at a reasonable cost. On the other hand, school districts with limited availability of bilingual personnel in teaching, supervisory and administrative positions experienced much higher costs in implementing the program.

Size. The number of students, particularly in bilingual education programs, tended to influence the cost of the program. Up to a point, the addition of pupils to a bilingual program diminishes the cost of the program on a per pupil basis. This phenomenon was constrained in that at some point the increased size of the program tends to produce a need for supervisory and administrative staff which produces a jump in per pupil costs which is, again, diminished by further pupil increases.

Areas of Expenditures

After analyzing a large number of areas of expenditures, project staff and the panel of experts determined that all significant expenditures for bilingual education were concentrated in only five areas of expenditures. The five areas of expenditures ranked from highest to lowest are presented below.

Staffing. As I stated previously, the cost of staffing a bilingual education program was largely influenced by the availability of bilingual staff in various personnel categories. Proposals to allow a compensatory factor for school districts not having bilingual personnel were rejected by project staff as favoring school districts which may have utilized discriminatory employment practices in the past.

The provision of additional instructional staff for bilingual education programs was deemed as an imperative for providing one-to-one pupil-to-teacher interactions for modeling in two languages. Though project staff and the panel exhibited wide disparities on their estimates of the amount of additional instructional staff required for minimally adequate bilingual programs, the study recommended that an additional staff of .30 per instructional unit or .30 additional personnel units for each 19-21 children (depending on the grade level involved) in average daily attendance. The project further recommended extensive flexibility in the allocation of the .30 additional personnel units which would allow a school system to employ bilingual paraprofessionals, additional teachers or supervisory and administrative units depending on the characteristics and needs of each school district. The cost of this additional staff amounted to approximately $160 per pupil per year in kindergarten, first grade, second grade and third grade, and $145 per pupil per year in grades four and five.

The staffing of preservice education and its inclusion in the costing of a bilingual education program is conspicuous by its absence. Preservice education was not included by the project because the costs of training teachers prior to service is not a normal cost borne by state or school systems. It is a cost in preparation for a bilingual education program, but not a cost in the operation of the program, and it is not a recurring cost once an adequate supply of bilingual education personnel is available. Neither the project staff nor the panel of experts intended to imply nor should it be inferred that the preservice training is not an essential need in bilingual education nor that state and local districts should default in the responsibility for providing an adequate cadre of educational personnel essential to the success of a bilingual education program. On the contrary, the project strongly recommends that the state address itself in a separate category to the need for preservice training of large numbers of teachers and other school personnel essential to the success of bilingual education efforts in the state.

Materials. The project identified a need for instructional classroom materials for bilingual education over and beyond materials and supplies generally made available in monolingual programs. The cost for this material was computed at between $11 per pupil per year and $35 per pupil per year depending on the grade level and year of implementation.

Library. The project identified a need for additional library resources in support of a bilingual education program. Using current accreditation standards, staff ascertained that a need for seven additional volumes per pupil in bilingual education classes for start-up purposes and an additional $9 per pupil per year in new purchases. The cost for these library resources was constant at $25 per pupil in the first year of implementation and $9 per pupil in each subsequent year.

Equipment. The cost analysis project identified a wide array of equipment which would be advantageous to a bilingual education program. However, when applying the comparability rule which assumes that a bilingual education program would be comparable to a monolingual program, almost all equipment, including audio-visual aids, was found to be equally essential to traditional programs as to the bilingual education programs. The only exception for additional equipment identified was a need for language masters which record and reproduce models of language which could be used extensively by students in the acquisition of a second language. Assuming that such equipment has an average life span of three years, costs were estimated at approximately $20 in kindergarten, first, second and third grades, and $10 in grades four and five. Replacement costs in subsequent years were estimated at almost $7 per pupil per year in kindergarten through third grade and $3.50 per pupil per year in grades four and five.

Testing. The implementation of a bilingual education program demands the utilization of additional tests. The Cost Analysis Project determined that assessment procedures and testing for the identification and assignment of students to a bilingual education program were part of general needs assessment expenditures which should be implemented for all pupils regardless of language characteristics and should not be attributed to a bilingual education program. The project did identify the need for two additional types of tests, a language proficiency test for determining language characteristics and needs of children entering a bilingual education program and the inclusion of one additional achievement test to determine bilingual education outcomes not generally included in school testing programs. The cost for testing materials and scoring ranged from $1.32 to almost $3 per pupil per year depending on the grade level and year of implementation.

The total cost of a bilingual education program in Texas was estimated as follows:

Bilingual Education Costs

Grade	*Year of Implementation*			
	One	Two	Three	Four
K	243.77	201.92	199.92	197.91
1	239.96	201.11	199.11	197.10
2	238.07	200.22	197.22	197.21
3	237.08	198.23	197.23	196.22
4	205.69	173.69	172.68	170.68
5	205.77	173.77	172.76	170.76

Weighted Pupil Factor

In order to allow for the utilization of the averages presented above in the bilingual education costs in a variety of school districts with high and low expenditure levels, the average costs were converted into a weighted pupil factor which indicates, on an index basis, the relationship between bilingual education costs and the cost of a comparable monolingual education program. The weighted pupil factors were computed on the basis of full time equivalency since all parties in the project were in agreement that a bilingual education program is a full time school activity and not an appendage to an existing program.

Weighted Pupil Factors for Bilingual Education

Grade	*Year of Implementation*			
	One	Two	Three	Four
K	1.31	1.25	1.25	1.25
1	1.42	1.35	1.35	1.34
2	1.41	1.35	1.34	1.34
3	1.41	1.35	1.34	1.34
4	1.36	1.30	1.30	1.30
5	1.36	1.30	1.30	1.30

CONCLUSIONS

The tables presented above produce two conclusions in addition to providing both absolute and relative costs for the implementation of bilingual education programs. The first conclusion is that the $45 per pupil per year being provided in Texas for the implementation of bilingual education programs is most inadequate to meet the needs of even a minimally adequate program. In a kindergarten classroom, during the first year of implementation, the amount provided by the state of Texas is less than one-fifth of the cost of a minimally adequate program. At best, at the intermediate grades (four and five) in the fourth year of implementation, the funds being provided comprise about 25 percent of the necessary funds. It has been no wonder that many school districts have been less than eager to comply with state and federal legislation and court orders demanding a bilingual education program for children of limited English speaking ability, when such legislation and court orders are accompanied by an appropriation which provides only 20 to 25 percent of the cost of the mandated programs. The alternatives available to school districts are either to provide a bogus, substandard program which may be misrepresented to meet the letter of the law, or fund the program almost entirely at local expense. Since IDRA has determined, in prior studies, that the Mexican American population in Texas and, therefore, children of limited English speaking ability, tend to reside in the poorest tax wealth districts of Texas, local financing of bilingual education is a dysfunctional alternative to inadequate programs. It is no wonder that many school district personnel have opted toward a third alternative, namely, opposing bilingual education on pedagogical, psychological and/or civic grounds, rather than assuming the cost with inadequate resources.

Recommendations

The Intercultural Development Research Association, understanding the temporal, personal and fiscal limitations of this study, makes a strong recommendation for further study in this area. IDRA and the Bilingual Education Cost Analysis Project strongly recommend that further studies undertake the following.

The replication of this study in other states in order to validate the weighted pupil factors and cost estimates derived in this study. This activity must be undertaken in states having large target populations of children of limited English speaking ability who have an urgent need for adequate bilingual education programs.

Additional studies be conducted in the area of preservice training for staff of bilingual education programs. Questions pertaining to where, how and how many are in desperate need of answers so that institutions of higher education may address their responsibilities in the training of instructional staff for bilingual education.

Further studies be conducted on the relationship between declining school enrollments in urban school districts and the need for additional bilingual education staff. The declining school enrollments, particularly in school districts with large minority populations, have necessitated reductions in instructional staff at the same time that the school district is needing new staff with the necessary training and competencies for the implementation of a bilingual education program.

Further study be conducted to determine the monitoring of needs of a bilingual education program. Minimum standards must be developed for the identification and enrollment of the target population, the variety of subject areas to be included in a bilingual program, culturally and linguistically relevant methodologies and the adequacy of curriculum materials and alternative organizational patterns.

Plans be developed for increasing school district accountability in dealing with children of limited English speaking ability. It is necessary that the school district determine the extent to which bilingual and other programs are meeting the needs of such children with maximum efficiency and effectiveness.

viewpoint: James Cummins

Psycholinguistic Evidence

Although the reviews in this series provide a comprehensive analysis of many of the important issues in bilingual education, I believe that neither individually nor collectively do they provide an adequate general model for the evaluation of bilingual education programs. This statement is based on the fact that issues of a psychological nature, which are fundamental to the very existence of bilingual education programs, have escaped the meshes of their respective nets.

The only "official" justification for the provision of bilingual education lies in the proposition that the academic progress of children of limited English speaking ability will be promoted more effectively if initial instruction is in their native language. This proposition immediately raises issues of a psychological nature concerning the developmental interrelations between a bilingual child's proficiency in his two languages, his cognitive development and his academic progress.

If we agree that a bilingual child's level of competence in L_1 and L_2 is relevant to his capacity to benefit cognitively and academically from instruction in either language, then certain questions present themselves. For example, is there a certain minimum or threshold level of L_2 competence which a child must attain in order to benefit optimally from L_2 instruction? What types of L_1 and L_2 skills must develop to keep pace with the demands of an increasingly abstract curriculum which requires formal operational modes of thought? To what extent is a bilingual child who has devel-

---

Editor's Note: Dr. Cummins' paper was originally presented at the final, "synthesis" conference. The editors feel that the content of his paper properly belongs with the education perspective, and therefore have included it here.

oped fluent surface skills in L_1 and L_2 also capable of carrying out complex cognitive operations (e.g., verbal analogies, mathematical problems) through his two languages? To what extent are L_1 and L_2 skills interdependent and what are the implications of possible interdependencies for cognitive and academic progress? In other words, do children who maintain and develop their L_1 in school develop higher or lower L_2 skills than those whose L_1 is replaced by their L_2, and to what extent do various patterns of L_1-L_2 relationships facilitate children's general cognitive and academic progress?

These questions are all related to the more general question: Under what socio-pedagogical conditions do different patterns of L_1 and L_2 abilities accelerate, or alternatively, retard a bilingual child's cognitive and academic progress? As Fishman (1977) points out, "we are still a long way from this kind of research on the socio-cognitive-emotional concomitants of bilingualism and bilingual education" and the issues are difficult to address empirically. However, the dynamics of children's development within bilingual education programs will never be understood unless we start to examine these issues.

In this paper I shall outline a general model for the evaluation of bilingual education programs which provides for an explicit examination of these psychological issues and attempts to integrate the evaluational priorities suggested or implied in the other reviews. The model derives from an attempt (Cummins, 1976A, 1977A) to reconcile the apparent inconsistencies in the results of studies which reported a negative association between bilingualism and verbal intelligence and academic skills, on the one hand (see reviews by Darcy, 1953; Jensen, 1962; Macnamara, 1966; Peal and Lambert, 1962), and more recent findings which suggest that bilingualism can positively influence cognitive functioning. These studies will be briefly considered and their implications for evaluations of bilingual education programs drawn out.

RECENT STUDIES OF THE COGNITIVE EFFECTS OF BILINGUALISM

Some recent studies support the earlier findings of negative cognitive and academic outcomes associated with bilingualism. In particular, Macnamara's (1966) study has been regarded as supporting a "negative theory of bilingualism (Stern, 1953)." Macnamara argued (a) that there is a "balance effect" in language learning, i.e. bilinguals paid for their L_2 skills by a decrease in L_1 skills and (b) that instruction in a weaker language led to retardation in problem arithmetic. A close examination of Macnamara's data, however, fails to support either of these conclusions.

The "balance effect" interpretation of Macnamara's

findings is difficult to sustain since the Irish immersion group (whose L_1 is English) performed at the same level in English reading as children instructed through English (their L_1) and taught Irish as a school subject. The fact that the *entire* national sample in Macnamara's study performed at a lower level than the norming British sample may be due to a number of cultural and curricular factors--one of which is that less time was spent on English instruction.

The limitations of using standardized reading tests as the sole measures of English and Irish competence should also be pointed out. Macnamara reported that the immersion group performed no better in Irish reading skills than regular program pupils. However, the recent Committee on Language Attitudes Research Report (1975) found that attendance at an Irish immersion school was a highly significant predictor of later Irish speaking ability and use of Irish. Thus, Macnamara's dependent measures may not have been sufficiently sensitive to the objectives of the Irish immersion schools.

Cummins (1977B) has argued that Macnamara's finding of lower problem arithmetic scores among the immersion group is uninterpretable since the effects of testing through a weaker language are confounded with the effects of instruction in a weaker language. Thus, the lower problem arithmetic scores of the immersion group could be due to either or both of these phenomena, but can be attributed unequivocably to neither.

Macnamara's (1966) findings have been considered in some detail not only because they continue to be misinterpreted (see for example, Trites, 1976; Trites and Price, 1975) but also because his study raises some extremely important issues. For example, what levels of L_2 competence are necessary to benefit optimally from instruction in L_2 and to perform complex cognitive operations in L_2? These issues underlie the interpretation of Macnamara's problem arithmetic data and their relevance for evaluations of bilingual education programs is considered in a later section.

The methodological deficiencies in two other recent studies which reported that bilingualism is associated with lower levels of cognitive skills are instructive. Tsushima and Hogan (1975) reported that grade four and five Japanese-English bilinguals performed at a significantly lower level on measures of verbal intelligence and academic skills than a unilingual group matched on nonverbal IQ. Although the authors report that the bilingual children had been exposed to both English and Japanese in the home from infancy, they give no details of the present pattern of bilinguals' usage in the home nor of the bilinguals' relative competence in both languages.

The same criticism can be made of a study conducted in Singapore by Torrance, Gowan, Wu and Aliotti (1970), who reported that bilingual children in grades three, four and five performed at a significantly lower level than unilingual children on the fluency and flexibility scales of the Torrance Tests of Creative Thinking. However, the trend was reversed on the originality and elaboration scales and differences in favor of the bilingual group on the elaboration scale were significant. Cummins (1977A) has suggested, on the basis of differences in divergent thinking between balanced and non-balanced bilinguals, that in the Torrance et al study, only children who had attained relatively fluent bilingual skills may have been at an advantage in originality and elaboration skills while the lower fluency and flexibility scores may be attributable only to those bilinguals who had failed to overcome difficulties in coping with two languages.

While the studies of Tsushima and Hogan (1975) and Torrance et al (1970) suggest that under some conditions bilingual learning experiences may have negative effects on certain cognitive skills, they tell us very little about what these conditions are or what patterns of L_1-L_2 competencies are associated with negative effects. This failure to provide information on bilinguals' linguistic competencies comes into focus when the contradictions between these negative findings and more recent positive findings are considered.

Some of these recent studies suggest that bilingualism can accelerate the development of general intellectual skills (Bain, 1975; Balkan, 1970; Cummins and Gulutsan, 1974; Liedke and Nelson, 1968; Peal and Lambert, 1962). There is also evidence that becoming bilingual promotes an analytic orientation to language (Ben-Zeev, 1972, 1975, 1976; Cummins, 1977C; Feldman and Shen, 1971; Ianco-Worrall, 1972). A positive association between bilingualism and divergent thinking has also been noted (Carringer, 1974; Cummins and Gulutsan, 1974; Scott, 1973) and several studies suggest that learning a second language increases children's sensitivity to feedback cues (Bain, 1975, 1976; Ben-Zeev, 1975; Cummins, 1976B).

Although, in general, these studies have been better controlled than the earlier studies which reported negative findings, few are without methodological defects. A problem in many of these studies (Bain, 1976; Carringer, 1974; Cummins and Gulutsan, 1974; Feldman and Shen, 1971; Peal and Lambert, 1962) is lack of adequate controls for possible background differences between bilingual and unilingual groups. An index of SES based on parental occupation provides inadequate protection against bias. Although the remaining studies have matched bilingual and unilingual groups on IQ in addition to SES, the validity of some of the dependent measures used to assess constructs such as "analytic orientation to language" or "sensitivity to feedback cues" has not been demonstrated. Thus, pending replication and extension, these findings should be evaluated cautiously so that, as Fishman (1977) warns "bilingualism will not be spuriously oversold now as it was spuriously undersold (or written off) in the past."

Despite the fact that these recent "positive" studies are not methodologically flawless, taken together they suggest that under some conditions, access to two languages in early childhood can accelerate aspects of cognitive growth. How do we reconcile this conclusion with findings of a negative association between bilingualism and verbal-academic tasks?

LINGUISTIC COMPETENCE AS A MEDIATING VARIABLE

Cummins (1976A) has hypothesized that the level of competence attained by a bilingual child in his two languages may act as an intervening variable in mediating the effects of his bilingual learning experiences on cognitive growth. This hypothesis attempts to resolve the apparent inconsistencies in the results of "positive" and "negative" studies and is derived from an analysis of methodological differences and differences in second language acquisition contexts between these two types of studies.

The methodological difference which is most relevant to specifying conditions under which bilingual learning experiences might exert a positive or negative influence on cognitive growth is related to procedures for choosing the bilingual sample. The majority of recent "positive" studies have taken precautions to ensure that the bilingual subjects were "balanced" bilinguals, i.e. had a similar (but not necessarily equal) degree of competence in both languages. In other words, bilinguals who were very much more dominant in one of their two languages were excluded from the bilingual sample. Studies which reported negative effects, on the other hand, failed to assess the bilingual subjects' relative degree of competence in their two languages.

Two points should be noted in relation to this methodological difference. First, while many recent studies suggest that "balanced" bilingualism may be associated with accelerated cognitive development, these studies tell us nothing about the cognitive growth of children who remain very dominant in one of their two languages. Second, a "balanced" bilingual may have either a high level of competence or a low level of competence in both languages. Thus, by itself, the fact that subjects in "positive" studies have been "balanced" provides only a partial picture of the linguistic competence of these subjects. In order to specify more precisely the differences in linguistic competence between the bilingual subjects in "positive" and "negative" studies, it is necessary to consider the language acquisition contexts in which these two types of studies have been carried out.

Lambert (1975) has suggested that "positive" and "negative" studies can be distinguished in terms of the "additiveness" and "subtractiveness" of the bilingual learning conditions under which subjects acquired their two languages. Many of the earlier "negative" studies involved bilingual subjects from language minority groups whose first language (L_1) was gradually being replaced by their second language (L_2, usually the dominant and more prestigious language). The bilingualism of these subjects is termed "subtractive" in that the bilingual's competence in his two languages at any point in time is likely to reflect some stage in the subtraction of the L_1 and its replacement by the L_2. Thus, it is not surprising that many of these earlier studies produced evidence of a "balance effect" (Macnamara, 1966) in language learning, i.e. that a bilingual paid for his L_2 competence by a lowering of L_1 competence. The lower levels of verbal intelligence of the bilingual subjects in these studies may be a reflection of the fact that many of them are likely to have had less than native-like competence in both their languages.

Recent "positive" studies, on the other hand, have generally involved middle or upper class subjects whose first language is dominant, or at least prestigious, and in no danger of replacement by their second language. In other words, as Lambert (1975) points out, these children are adding another language to their repertory of skills. The evidence from bilingual education programs in such "additive" settings indicates that children generally achieve high levels of L_2 competence at no cost to their L_1 (e.g., Cohen, 1975; Lambert and Tucker, 1972; Swain, 1974).

A combination of the methodological differences and differences in language acquisition contexts between "positive" and "negative" studies leads to the conclusion that qualitative differences exist in the linguistic competence attained by bilingual subjects in each of these two types of studies. The balanced bilingual subjects in "positive" studies carried out in additive environments are likely to have achieved a high level of L_2 competence at no cost to their L_1. Many of the bilingual subjects in "negative" studies, carried out in subtractive environments, on the other hand, may have had less than native-like skill in both their languages.

This analysis suggests that the level of competence a bilingual child achieves in his two languages may mediate the effects of his bilingual learning experiences on cognition. Developing this idea in the context of immersion education programs, Cummins (1976A, 1977A) has suggested that there may be a threshold level of linguistic competence which a bilingual child must attain both in order to avoid cognitive deficits and to allow the potentially beneficial aspects of becoming bilingual to influence his cognitive growth.

What are the implications of the threshold hypothesis for evaluations of bilingual education programs? An immediate implication is that evaluations of such programs should examine the effects of the program on cognition not only for the group as a whole but also separately for those who have attained and those who have failed to attain a high level of functional bilingualism. The very different level of cognitive performance of these two groups might mask each other when the performance of only the total group is considered. Initial research findings (Barik and Swain, 1976; Cummins, 1977A) are consistent with the general hypothesis and suggest that children in immersion programs who achieve high levels of functional bilingualism may experience cognitive advantages.

A MODEL FOR EVALUATING BILINGUAL EDUCATION PROGRAMS

The preceding analysis suggests that a bilingual child's levels of competence in L_1 and L_2 be regarded not only as static outcome variables, but also as *process* variables which mediate the cognitive and academic outcomes of schooling. The model implied by this hypothesis is radically different from the implicit models which underlie current evaluations of bilingual education programs. The implicit model used in the vast majority of bilingual education (BE) programs has involved treating the BE program as an independent variable and comparing its academic outcomes with those of ESL or "regular" school programs. This model is represented by: BE programs ⟶ academic outcomes.

Several writers (e.g., Fishman, 1977; Paulston, 1977) have argued that this model is inadequate in that BE programs cannot be treated in isolation from the socio-cultural context that gave rise to them. Paulston especially has argued that apparently contradictory findings can be reconciled only when they are considered as the *result* of societal factors rather than independent variables in their own right. These considerations give rise to the following evaluational model which is implied in the reviews in this series: societal factors ⟶ BE programs ⟶ academic outcomes.

However, this model too is inadequate in that it fails to consider variables of a "process" nature which intervene between program input and academic output. The rationale for BE explicitly raises the question of the developmental interrelationships of language and thought. Yet this issue cannot be considered within the context of present evaluational models. Based on the synthesis of studies of the cognitive development of bilingual children the following model is suggested.

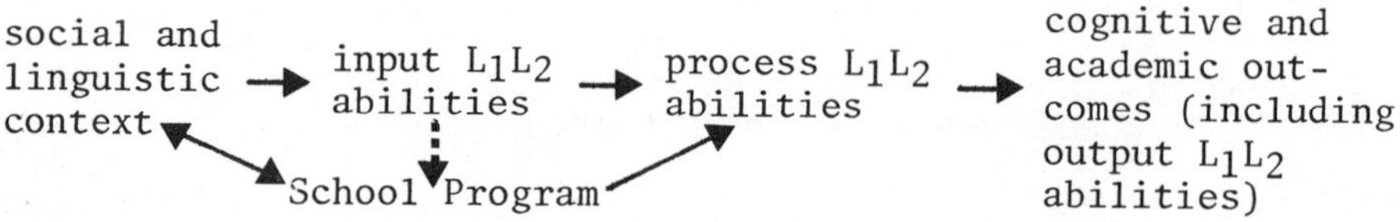

The essential attribute of this model is that a bilingual child's L_1 and L_2 abilities are considered not only as outcome variables of particular school programs but also as (a) process variables which mediate cognitive and academic outcomes and (b) independent variables (in relation to the school program) which ought to (hence the broken arrow) determine the appropriate form of educational intervention.

The social and linguistic context refers to those factors which contribute to the additiveness or subtractiveness of particular bilingual learning situations. Especially important and emphasized by both Paulston (1977) and Fishman (1977) are the values and attitudes of both minority and majority language groups. Also included are factors such as the extent of L_1 and L_2 use in the home and community, age of exposure to L_2, etc. These social and linguistic factors are posited to directly determine the level of L_1 and L_2 competence of the child when he enters school.

The present model is similar to the models implied by Fishman (1977) and Paulston (1977) in that bilingual (or other) school programs are regarded as the result of particular constellations of societal variables rather than independent variables in their own right. Reciprocal influences are posited in the present model to allow for the possibility that the initiation of a bilingual program can affect the community's attitude towards language maintenance or language learning. This has been the case in many recently initiated immersion programs in Ireland.

Clearly, the most directly relevant question facing bilingual education today is, given certain constellations of social-linguistic factors and input L_1-L_2 abilities, what forms of educational intervention will optimally promote cognitive and academic outcomes? The present model implies that in order to answer this question we must reorient our research efforts and focus on children's L_1 and L_2 abilities as intervening variables which mediate cognitive and academic outcomes. L_1 and L_2 abilities must be evaluated as *process* variables rather than as static outcome variables. In other words, the model explicitly raises *psychological* questions which are essential for an understanding of the cognitive development and academic performance of minority language children. It focuses research on the relationships between a bilingual child's competence in L_1 and L_2 and on the extent to which the child can operate cognitively in each language. Even Piagetian theory, which takes a conservative position on the developmental interrelationships of language and thought, admits that language is probably necessary for the development of formal operational thought (about age 12). Consequently, the facility with which a bilingual child can utilize the symbolic system of each language to express and develop his thought is a relevant consideration in explaining his academic performance.

How is the process nature of L_1 and L_2 abilities to be measured? The relevant questions must first be formulated. Some questions which are central to the very existence of bilingual education programs are: What levels of L_1 or L_2 abilities are necessary to profit from instruction in L_1 or L_2? What levels of L_1 or L_2 abilities are necessary to carry out complex cognitive operations in L_1 or L_2? How is the ability to assimilate subject matter content in L_1 or L_2 related to the ability to operate cognitively through L_1 or L_2? To what extent, and in what ways, are L_1 and L_2 abilities interdependent?

The teaching strategies in bilingual education programs are based on implicit assumptions about these and other similar issues. Until these assumptions are made explicit and research conducted to test their validity, the implementation of bilingual education programs is likely to proceed in a blind trial and error fashion.

The relevance of this type of question can be illustrated by a recent debate between Cummins (1977B) and Macnamara regarding the interpretation of Macnamara's (1966) finding of a lower level of problem arithmetic competence among children in Irish immersion schools. The issue in the debate concerns the third question outlined above. Macnamara's argument implied that if children's Irish competence is such that they are handicapped on an Irish version of the problem arithmetic test then they are unlikely to optimally benefit from instruction through Irish. Cummins' position, on the other hand, implies that different linguistic abilities may underlie these two phenomena and inferior performance on a test administered in a weaker language does not necessarily imply inferior assimilation of instructional content taught in that language.

This dispute suggests a potentially sensitive way of measuring the deeper or cognitive components of a bilingual's linguistic competence. The extent to which a child is capable of carrying out complex cognitive operations (e.g., verbal analogies, mathematical problems) through his two languages may provide an index of his relative abilities in both languages and their relationships to his cognitive competence. Only if a child performs at a low level on culturally and educationally appropriate measures in both languages are inferences regarding inferior cognitive or subject matter competence justified. However, a child's performance in a particular language may provide a measure of his competence in the cognitive aspects of that language. As Shuy (n.d.) points out, the critical variables in assessing the cognitive component of L_1 and L_2 abilities are likely to be those which are less quantifiable and testable, i.e. semantic and functional meaning. As we shall see, fluent "surface" skills of production and comprehension may constitute only a "linguistic facade" and need not imply adequate linguistic skills at a cognitive level.

These psychological issues which are explicitly raised in the proposed model are easily overlooked in alternative models. Although the empirical problems are complex, these issues cannot be ignored if we are to understand the dynamics of the development of minority language children within bilingual or regular school programs.

The final section will attempt to demonstrate the heuristic value of the proposed model by consideration of an investigation whose approach was very similar to that advocated here. The findings of the Finnish National Commission Report to UNESCO (Skutnabb-Kangas and Toukomaa, 1976) provide partial answers to the fourth question posed above (the extent of the interdependence of L_1 and L_2) and have important implications for bilingual education in the United States. I shall try to show how the theoretical framework of the UNESCO investigation is similar to that proposed here and how it is capable of generating important and usually neglected questions. The purpose of the UNESCO investigation (Skutnabb-Kangas and Toukomaa, 1976)

> was to determine the linguistic level and development in both their mother tongue and Swedish of Finnish migrant children attending Swedish comprehensive school. Above all, attention was paid to the interdependence between skills in the mother tongue and Swedish, i.e. the hypothesis was tested that those who have best preserved their mother tongue are also best in Swedish.

This hypothesis was strongly supported by the findings. Although the Finnish migrant children had average levels of nonverbal intellectual ability, their skills in both Finnish and Swedish were considerably below Finnish and Swedish norms. The extent to which the mother tongue had been developed prior to contact with Swedish was strongly related to how well Swedish was learned. Children who migrated at age 10 maintained a level of Finnish close to Finnish students in Finland and achieved Swedish language skills comparable to those of Swedes. Skutnabb-Kangas and Toukomaa (1976) point out that "their skills in the mother tongue have already developed to the abstract level. For this reason they reach a better level in the mastery of Swedish-language concepts in quite a short time than those who moved before or at the start of school, and before long surpass even the migrant children who were born in Sweden."

The situation is very different for children who were seven-eight years of age when they moved to Sweden. "The verbal development of these children, who moved just as school was beginning, underwent serious disturbance after the move. This also has a detrimental effect on learning Swedish. In this group, and in those who moved before starting school, the risk of becoming semi-lingual is greatest."

Notice that the L_1 and L_2 abilities of the migrant children are considered within the context of their overall conceptual development. This emphasis is made explicit in the notion of "semilingualism." Skutnabb-Kangas and Toukomaa point out that research which viewed semilingualism as a purely linguistic variable found little support for the concept. However, research which supported the existence of semilingualism "measured cognitive aspects of the language, understanding of the meanings of abstract concepts, synonyms, etc. as well as vocabulary."

These cognitive aspects of the language are related to Hansegard's qualitative characteristics of linguistic skills: (a) ability to create or neologize; (b) mastery of cognitive, emotional and volitional functions of the language; and (c) richness or poorness in individual meanings, e.g. whether reading or listening to a particular linguistic system evokes lively and differential semantic images or not (Skutnabb-Kangas and Toukomaa, 1976).

The authors point out that semilingualism cannot "be used as a strictly linguistic concept at all." Although parents, teachers and the children themselves consider Finnish migrant children's Swedish to be quite fluent, tests in Swedish which require complex cognitive operations to be carried out show that this surface fluency is to a certain extent a "linguistic facade." The concept of semilingualism, and its cognitive nature, implies that assessments of L_1 and L_2 abilities of minority language children ought to measure the extent to which a child is capable of carrying out complex cognitive operations in both his languages. Such an assessment may provide sensitive indices of a child's cognitive competence in both languages. The relationships between these deeper levels of cognitive-linguistic competence and surface fluency need to be investigated, as does the extent to which each type of linguistic ability is influenced by different educational programs and, in turn, influences achievement in these programs.

As in the model outlined above, Skutnabb-Kangas and Toukomaa emphasize that semilingualism is an intervening variable which mediates between societal variables and school outcomes. It should not be treated as a deficiency within the child which "explains" his poor school achievement. Rather, semilingualism is a result both of societal factors and the failure of the educational system to meet the migrant child's needs by actively promoting the development of his mother tongue.

One should avoid simplistic generalizations of the findings of the UNESCO report to the North American context. It is salutary to recall that somewhat different forms of educational treatment are implied for the four groups who migrated at different ages. For example, for children who moved at age 10, the present system may be adequate and special emphasis on mother tongue maintenance may not be required. For these pupils and those who moved at age 12, the language acquisition context may be more additive than subtractive. Maintenance programs, however, are clearly implied for the two younger age groups (moved at seven-eight years and under six years). In fact, the subtractive nature of the bilingual learning situation may be so strong that only preschool literacy in L_1, as advocated by Christian (1976), may be adequate to provide a basis for acquisition of Swedish and full development of both languages.

Despite the necessity to avoid simplistic generalizations, it is clear that both the findings and theoretical framework of the UNESCO report are relevant to bilingual education in the United States. A research focus on the development of L_1 and L_2 skills (both "surface" and "deep") viewed as intervening variables which mediate between societal and educational influences on the one hand, and cognitive and academic outcomes on the other, will provide a much more adequate rationale for intervention by means of bilingual education programs than has existed hitherto. Children's cognitive development and academic progress within bilingual programs must be considered *not* as a function of the program itself but as a function of children's L_1 and L_2 abilities which are determined by the *interaction* between a particular program, the socio-cultural context within which it operates and the level and depth of children's L_1 and L_2 competence on entry to the program. Evaluations which ignore this interaction and aggregate data from different types of bilingual programs, operating under different socio-cultural conditions and catering to children with varying levels of input L_1 and L_2 abilities are likely to be uninterpretable.

viewpoint: Joseph D. Garcia

Analyzing Bilingual Education Costs

The primary intent of the various state statutes on bilingual education has been to provide equal educational opportunities to the limited English speaking and non-English speaking child. The language of the bilingual state statutes implies a legislative commitment toward bilingual education. However, if one goes beyond the legislative rhetoric of the statutes, it becomes obvious that the legislative commitment toward bilingual education is, at best, peripheral. This observation is based on the fact that the various state legislatures fail to appropriate the needed funds to adequately implement the bilingual education programs required to satisfy the needs of the limited English speaking and non-English speaking students.

As of 1976, New Mexico was the only state that funded bilingual education as part of its cost differential funding formula. Other states funded bilingual education categorically and still many other states provided no state monies for bilingual education. Studies comparing the cost of bilingual education to nonbilingual education programs are necessary to determine policy formation and appropriations required to adequately meet the bilingual needs of students.

The purpose of the Bilingual Multicultural Education Act as enacted by the 1973 New Mexico State Legislature is to ensure equal educational opportunities for students in New Mexico. At their discretion, local school districts may submit to the Department of Education a proposal for bilingual education programs. To be eligible for state financial support, each bilingual program must meet certain specified requirements as stipulated by the Department of Education. The guidelines require that each program:*

**Public School Code and Miscellaneous Provisions Affecting the Public Schools of the State of New Mexico*. Indianapolis, IN: Allen Smith, Co., 1975.

1. Provide for the educational needs of linguistically and culturally different students... with priority to be given to programs in grades K through three...for which there is an identifiable need to improve the language capabilities of these students before funding programs at higher grade levels.

2. Use two languages as mediums of instruction for any part or all of the curriculum.

3. Use teachers who have specialized in elementary education and who have received special training in bilingual education conducted through the use of two languages.

4. Emphasize the history and cultures associated with the students' mother tongue.

ONE STUDY TO DETERMINE BILINGUAL EDUCATION PROGRAM COSTS

Objectives

The present study was designed to (a) determine the program costs for bilingual education programs operating in New Mexico school districts during the 1974-75 school year; (b) compare and analyze the bilingual education program costs to the nonbilingual regular education program costs; (c) determine the add-on or extra costs associated with bilingual education; and (d) determine the add-on cost index for bilingual education.

Summary

Data was collected from all 88 school districts in New Mexico, and revealed that 62 districts, or 70 percent, provided bilingual programs. The findings show that it costs 27 percent of the regular education program cost per pupil to provide bilingual education programs beyond the regular education program. The add-on expenditures incurred in the 27 percent (0.27 add-on cost index) reflect the added or extra expenditures for teacher aides, program administration and supplies which were directly spent for bilingual education programs that go beyond the regular education program. Only state-funded programs were included in the study.

The study determined only the costs of the bilingual education programs as they existed in the 62 New Mexico school districts providing such programs during the 1974-75 school year. It *does not* reflect costs associated with the quality of the programs. The pioneer efforts of this study are by no means completed. More comprehensive studies in the area of bilingual education program costs are essential.

Recommendations

No attempt is made to relate the findings of this study to school districts of other states. However, the procedures used here are applicable to other states conducting cost studies in bilingual education programs. The following research efforts relative to bilingual education program costs are strongly recommended.

A study to determine the costs associated with different bilingual education program delivery systems, i.e. transitional vs. language maintenance model.

A study to compare the spending patterns of Title VII federally-funded bilingual education programs to state-funded bilingual education programs.

Cost effectiveness studies for bilingual education programs which are considered successful.

States providing bilingual education programs should conduct studies to determine the relative costs of their bilingual education programs.

METHODOLOGY OF THE NEW MEXICO STUDY

Data Collection

Two data collection instruments were designed to collect the data relative to bilingual education and nonbilingual regular education programs. *Section V of Data Collection Instrument No. 2* was designed to collect data relative to bilingual education programs in New Mexico (see page 93). This instrument was field-tested in selected New Mexico school districts for purposes of refining the instrument in terms of item clarity and availability of data in the format requested.

Per pupil expenditures in the regular school program, grades four to six, for each of the public school districts were determined. Program costs per pupil in the regular education program provide base line data for comparing the costs of other educational programs.

The regular education program consists of instructional activities provided to students enrolled in grades four to six. Section 77-6-18.3 of the Public School Code of the State of New Mexico established grades four to six as the regular education program to serve as the base with a cost index of 1.00. Cost indices for all other education programs are relative to that regular education program.

Program costs per pupil for each of the bilingual education and the regular education programs were determined by computing the total expenditures for each program and dividing by the number of FTE (full-time equivalent) or ADM (average daily membership) students served in that program.

All operational expenditures were included in calculating

Data Collection Instrument No. 2

District Code No. ________ (Leave Blank)

Section V, Bilingual Education

All questions are to be answered for Operational funded FTE's, Salaries and Other Expenditures except where otherwise specified for the fiscal year 1974-75. Expenditure information must correspond to Monthly Budget Report: 1974-75 for the month of June 1975, column 7, entitled "Total Expended To Date." Full-time equivalents (FTE) personnel must correspond to Report of Average Salaries 1974-75: Operational Budget Personnel Only, column 5. Some FTE and expenditure information is required from the 2200, Special Projects, series and is so designated. Expenditure account code numbers are designated for all questions in brackets either immediately following the question or underneath the blank to be filled in. When an expenditure account code number is not designated for a particular question, a column is left blank for you to insert the appropriate expenditure account code number for which a series of questions must be answered. If your district does not have FTE personnel and/or expenditures for a particular question, enter "N" for none in each appropriate blank. ALL QUESTIONS MUST BE ANSWERED.

	Operational FTE		Non-operational Federal Funded FTE		
1. Number of FTE classroom teachers serving Bilingual Education Programs in each of the respective educational program categories:	270 ____ 210.04	+	271 ____ 2200	=	272 ____ FTE Total
2. Number of FTE teacher aides serving Bilingual Education Programs in each of the respective educational program categories:	273 ____ 210.09	+	274 ____ 2200	=	275 ____ FTE Total

3. Number of FTE and salaries for Bilingual Education Program Administration by the following categories:

	Expend. Acct. Code Number		Oper. Salaries Paid		Categorical Federal Funded Salaries Paid
a. Program Administrator/Director	276 ____	277 ____	278 ____	279 ____ (2200)	280 ____ (2200)
b. Assistants/Coordinators/Others	281 ____	282 ____	283 ____	284 ____ (2200)	285 ____ (2200)
c. Secretarial/Clerical	286 ____	287 ____	288 ____	289 ____ (2200)	290 ____ (2200)

4. Number of FTE students served by operational and federal funds. (Use 40 or 80 Day reporting period information whichever was used for funding purposes).

291 ____ State Equalization FTE + 292 ____ Other Oper. FTE + 293 ____ Federal FTE = 294 ____ Total FTE

5. Total expenditures for Bilingual Education Program instructional supplies (220.01 + 220.02 + 230.01 + 240.01)

295 ____ Expenditures

Person completing Section V : ____________________ (Print or Type) Signature: ____________________

Position: ____________________ (Print or Type) Phone: ____________ District Name: ____________________ (Print or Type) per pupil costs. Indirect operational expenditures--those not directly related to a specific education program--were prorated to each program on the basis of either teachers or students. Because teachers served as a better workload indicator, expenditures for administration and operation and maintenance of plant were prorated on that basis since these types of expenditures are more closely related to teachers than students. Direct operational expenditures related to a specific educational program were computed as part of the per pupil costs for that particular program.

Pupil Expenditures for Regular Education Programs

Many calculations were required to determine the per pupil expenditures for the regular education program. Four worksheets, *I-A*, *I-B*, *I-C* and *I-D*, were developed by the researcher to determine the per pupil expenditures for grades four to six (see pages 95-99). The numbers refer to particular data items in the data collection instruments. A legend is provided for each worksheet to define the calculations.

Per Pupil Expenditures for Bilingual Education Programs

Worksheet II was designed by the researcher to determine the per pupil expenditures for bilingual education programs (see page 100). Section V of Data Collection Instrument No. 2 provided most of the data for the calculations in Worksheet II.

Expenditures for teacher salaries were determined by multiplying the number of FTE (full-time equivalent) teachers times the average teacher salary for the district plus the expenditures for substitute salaries. This figure is represented by *Item* A_2.

The total number of FTE students in bilingual education programs was determined by adding the number of FTE students funded specifically by the cost differential funding formula and other operational funds. The total number of FTE students is represented by *Item* A_3.

Expenditures for teacher aide salaries were determined by multiplying the number of FTE teacher aides times the average teacher aide salary for the district. Such expenditures were represented by *Item C*. Other direct expenditures for bilingual education programs included expenditures for program administration, coordinators, secretarial/clerical and instructional supplies.

Indirect expenditures for bilingual education programs included expenditures for general district-wide administration and for operation and maintenance of plant as represented by *Items* E_1 and *T*, respectively. The above expenditures were prorated on the basis of teachers.

Some New Mexico school districts received federal cate-

WORKSHEET I-A

DETERMINATION OF PER PUPIL EXPENDITURES FOR REGULAR EDUCATIONAL PROGRAMS, GRADES 4-6

Administration (100)

Total Items: 77 + 80 + 83 = _____ (A).

Total Items: 100 + 101 = _____ (B), Item 101 ÷ _____ (B) = _____ (C).

_____ (A) x _____ (C) = _____ (D).

Total Items: (113 + 116 + 119 + 153 + 158 + 163 + 237 + 242 + 247 + 278 + 288 + 303 + 308 + 313 if 100 Series or 210.01 is stated in the expenditure account code number) = _____ (E).

Total Items: 20 + 22 + 24 + 26 + 27 + 41 = _____ (F).

_____ (F) - _____ (A) + _____ (E) = _____ (G) ÷ Item B, Worksheet I-B =

_____ (H) x Item 101 = _____ (I) + _____ (D) = _____ (J).

_____ (J) ÷ Item 3 = _____ (K).

A = Expenditures for administration for grades 1-6

B = Total FTE teachers grades 1-6

C = Percent FTE teachers in grades 4-6

D = Expenditures for administration for grades 4-6 specified by proration

E = Expenditures for administration specified in other educational programs

F = Expenditures for administration including principals district-wide

G = Expenditures for administration district-wide unspecified

H = Per teacher expenditures for administration district-wide unspecified

I = Expenditures for administration grades 4-6 portion of unspecified

J = Total expenditures for administration grades 4-6

K = Per pupil expenditures for administration for grades 4-6

WORKSHEET I-B

<u>Instruction (200) and Attendance Services (300)</u>

Total Items: 91 + 95 + 99 = $\underset{A}{\_\_\_\_\_}$. Total Items: 28 + 31 = $\underset{B}{\_\_\_\_\_}$.

Total Items: 102 + 103 + 104a + 105a + 138 + 139 + 140a + 141a + 325a = $\underset{B_1}{\_\_\_\_\_}$.

Total Items: 29 + 32 = $\underset{C}{\_\_\_\_\_}$ - $\underset{B_1}{\_\_\_\_\_}$ = $\underset{C_1}{\_\_\_\_\_}$.

$\underset{C}{\_\_\_\_\_}$ + $\underset{B}{\_\_\_\_\_}$ = $\underset{D}{\_\_\_\_\_}$ x Item 101 = $\underset{E}{\_\_\_\_\_}$.

Item 3 + Item 101 = $\underset{F}{\_\_\_\_\_}$. $\underset{B}{\_\_\_\_\_}$ - Item 177 = $\underset{F_1}{\_\_\_\_\_}$.

Total Items: 37 + 54 = $\underset{I}{\_\_\_\_\_}$, Total Items: 38 + 55 = $\underset{J}{\_\_\_\_\_}$.

$\underset{J}{\_\_\_\_\_}$ + $\underset{I}{\_\_\_\_\_}$ = $\underset{K}{\_\_\_\_\_}$ x Item 108 = $\underset{L}{\_\_\_\_\_}$ + Item 3 = $\underset{M}{\_\_\_\_\_}$.

Item 58 ÷ $\underset{F_1}{\_\_\_\_\_}$ = $\underset{N}{\_\_\_\_\_}$ x Item 101 = $\underset{O}{\_\_\_\_\_}$.

$\underset{E}{\_\_\_\_\_}$ + $\underset{O}{\_\_\_\_\_}$ + Item 105a + Item 103 = $\underset{P}{\_\_\_\_\_}$ + Item 3 = $\underset{Q}{\_\_\_\_\_}$.

Total Items: 89 + 91 + 125 + 127 + (any corresponding expenditure where 210.03 is stated in the expenditure account code number) = $\underset{S}{\_\_\_\_\_}$.

Item 43 - $\underset{S}{\_\_\_\_\_}$ = $\underset{T}{\_\_\_\_\_}$ + $\underset{B}{\_\_\_\_\_}$ = $\underset{U}{\_\_\_\_\_}$ x Item 101 = $\underset{V}{\_\_\_\_\_}$.

Total Items: 45 + 47 + 49 + 51 = $\underset{W}{\_\_\_\_\_}$.

Total Items: 93 + 95 + 129 + 131 + 188 + 190 + 192 + 197 + 199 + 201 + 206 + 208 + 210 and any corresponding expenditure where 210.5 series is stated in the expenditure account code number = $\underset{X}{\_\_\_\_\_}$.

$\underset{W}{\_\_\_\_\_}$ - $\underset{X}{\_\_\_\_\_}$ = $\underset{Y}{\_\_\_\_\_}$ + Item 1 = $\underset{Z}{\_\_\_\_\_}$ x Item 3 = $\underset{AA}{\_\_\_\_\_}$.

Total Items: 97 + 99 + 133 + 135 + (any corresponding expenditure where 210.07 is stated in the expenditure account code number) = $\underset{BB}{\_\_\_\_\_}$.

Item 53 - $\underset{BB}{\_\_\_\_\_}$ = $\underset{CC}{\_\_\_\_\_}$ + Item 1 = $\underset{DD}{\_\_\_\_\_}$ x Item 3 = $\underset{EE}{\_\_\_\_\_}$.

Total Items: 109 + 145 + 146 + (172 if 170 = 220.01, 220.02, 230.01, or 240.01) + 212 + 214 + 216 + 218 + 295 + 321 = $\underset{FF}{\_\_\_\_\_}$.

Item 60 - (Item 110 + $\underset{FF}{\_\_\_\_\_}$) = $\underset{GG}{\_\_\_\_\_}$ + Item 1 = $\underset{HH}{\_\_\_\_\_}$.

$\underset{HH}{\_\_\_\_\_}$ x Item 3 = $\underset{II}{\_\_\_\_\_}$ + Item 110 = $\underset{JJ}{\_\_\_\_\_}$ + Item 3 = $\underset{KK}{\_\_\_\_\_}$.

$\underset{A}{\_\_\_\_\_}$ + $\underset{L}{\_\_\_\_\_}$ + $\underset{P}{\_\_\_\_\_}$ + $\underset{V}{\_\_\_\_\_}$ + $\underset{AA}{\_\_\_\_\_}$ + $\underset{EE}{\_\_\_\_\_}$ + $\underset{JJ}{\_\_\_\_\_}$ = $\underset{LL}{\_\_\_\_\_}$ + Item 3 = $\underset{MM}{\_\_\_\_\_}$.

A = Expenditures for instructional salaries excluding teacher and instructional aides salaries

B = Total teachers district-wide

B_1 = Total expenditures for teachers' increments and extended contracts

C = Total teachers' salaries district-wide

C_1 = Total teachers' salaries district-wide minus increments and extended contracts

D = Average teacher salary district-wide

E = Expenditures for teacher salaries grades 4-6

F = Pupil/teacher ratio

F_1 = Total teachers minus teachers in Class B programs

I = Total instructional aides district-wide

J = Total instructional aides salaries district-wide

K = Average instructional aide salary district-wide

L = Expenditures for instructional aide salaries grades 4-6

M = Per pupil expenditures for instructional aide salaries grades 4-6

N = Substitute salaries per FTE teacher district-wide

O = Substitute salaries expenditures grades 4-6

P = Total expenditures for teacher salaries grades 4-6

Q = Per pupil expenditures for teacher salaries grades 4-6

S = Total expenditures for coordinators specified

T = Expenditures for coordinators district-wide unspecified

U = Per teacher expenditures for coordinators district-wide unspecified

V = Expenditures for coordinators portion of unspecified for grades 4-6

W = Expenditures for other instructional personnel district-wide

X = Total expenditures for other instructional personnel specified

Y = Expenditures for other instructional personnel district-wide unspecified

Z = Per pupil expenditures for other instructional personnel district-wide unspecified

AA = Expenditures for other instructional personnel portion of unspecified for grades 4-6

BB = Expenditures for secretarial/clerical assistants specified

CC = Expenditures for secretarial/clerical assistants unspecified

DD = Per pupil expenditures for secretarial/clerical assistants unspecified

EE = Expenditures for secretarial/clerical assistants portion of unspecified for grades 4-6

FF = Expenditures for instructional supplies specified

GG = Expenditures for instructional supplies district-wide unspecified

HH = Per pupil expenditures for instructional supplies district-wide unspecified

II = Expenditures for instructional supplies grades 4-6 portion unspecified

JJ = Total expenditures for instructional supplies grades 4-6

KK = Per pupil expenditures for instructional supplies

LL = Total expenditures for instruction and attendance services grades 4-6

MM = Per pupil expenditures for instruction and attendance services grades 4-6

WORKSHEET I-C

Health Services (400), Operation (600) and Maintenance of Plant (700), Fixed Charges (800), and Student Activities (1000)

Total Items: 62 + 63 = ______ (A) + Item 1 = ______ (B) x Item 3 = ______ (C).

Item B, Worksheet I-B - Item 176 = ______ (C_1).

Total Items: 65 + 66 = ______ (D) + ______ (C_1) = ______ (E) x Item 101 = ______ (F).

Total Items: 68 + 69 = ______ (G) ÷ ______ (C_1) = ______ (H) x Item 101 = ______ (I).

Item 1 - Item 6 = ______ (J).

Item 70 ÷ ______ (J) = ______ (K) x Item 3 = ______ (L).

Item 71 + Item 1 = ______ (M) x Item 3 = ______ (N).

Total Items: 72 + 73 + 74 = ______ (O) x .125 = ______ (P).

______ (C) + ______ (F) + ______ (I) + ______ (L) + ______ (N) + ______ (P) = ______ (Q) ÷ Item 3 = ______ (R).

A = Total expenditures for health services district-wide

B = Per pupil expenditures for health services district-wide

C = Expenditures for health services grades 4-6

C_1 = Total FTE teachers minus Class A program FTE teachers

D = Total expenditures for operation of plant district-wide

E = Per teacher expenditures for operation of plant district-wide

F = Expenditures for operation of plant grades 4-6

G = Total expenditures for maintenance of plant district-wide

H = Per teacher expenditures for maintenance of plant district-wide

I = Expenditures for maintenance of plant grades 4-6

J = School district ADM excluding Early Childhood Education student FTE

K = Fixed charges (employee benefits) per pupil district-wide

L = Expenditures for (employee benefits) grades 4-6

M = Fixed charges (other) per pupil district-wide

N = Expenditures for fixed charges (other) grades 4-6

O = Expenditures for student activities district-wide

P = Expenditures for student activities grades 4-6

Q = Total expenditures for health services, operation & maintenance of plant, fixed charges, and student services grades 4-6

R = Per pupil expenditures for the above educational functions grades 4-6

WORKSHEET I-D

Total: From Worksheet I-A, Item K = _____

From Worksheet I-B, Item MM = _____

From Worksheet I-C, Item R = _____

_____ S

Sparsity Corrections

Total Items: 2 + 3 + 4 + 9 + 10 = _____ (T).

Item 14 + _____ (T) = _____ (U).

Item 1 - Item 6 = _____ (V).

Item 18 ÷ _____ (V) = _____ (W).

_____ (U) + _____ (W) = _____ (X).

_____ (S) - _____ (X) = _____ (Y).

S = Per pupil operational expenditures for grades 4-6

T = Total elementary, junior high, Special Education Classes C & D ADM

U = Per pupil allocations for elementary and junior high sparsity

V = School district ADM excluding Early Childhood Education student FTE

W = Per pupil allocations for district sparsity

X = Total per pupil allocations for sparsity

Y = Per pupil operational expenditures for grades 4-6, excluding sparsity

WORKSHEET II

DETERMINATION OF PER PUPIL EXPENDITURES FOR BILINGUAL EDUCATIONAL PROGRAMS

Item 270 x Item D, Worksheet I-B $\underset{A}{\underline{\hspace{3em}}}$.

Total Items: 11 + 292 = $\underset{A_3}{\underline{\hspace{3em}}}$.

Item 270 x Item N, Worksheet I-B = $\underset{A_1}{\underline{\hspace{3em}}}$ + $\underset{A}{\underline{\hspace{3em}}}$ = $\underset{A_2}{\underline{\hspace{3em}}}$.

$\underset{A_2}{\underline{\hspace{3em}}}$ + $\underset{A_3}{\underline{\hspace{3em}}}$ = $\underset{B}{\underline{\hspace{3em}}}$. $\underset{A_3}{\underline{\hspace{3em}}}$ + Item 270 = $\underset{B_1}{\underline{\hspace{3em}}}$.

Item 273 x Item K, Worksheet I-B = $\underset{C}{\underline{\hspace{3em}}}$ + $\underset{A_3}{\underline{\hspace{3em}}}$ = $\underset{D}{\underline{\hspace{3em}}}$.

Total Items: 278 + 283 + 288 = $\underset{E}{\underline{\hspace{3em}}}$.

Item H, Worksheet I-A x Item 270 = $\underset{E_1}{\underline{\hspace{3em}}}$.

Total Items: 280 + 285 + 290 = $\underset{F}{\underline{\hspace{3em}}}$. Item 270 ÷ Item 272 = $\underset{G}{\underline{\hspace{3em}}}$.

Item U, Worksheet I-B x Item 270 = $\underset{H}{\underline{\hspace{3em}}}$.

Items (291 + 292) ÷ Item 294 = $\underset{I}{\underline{\hspace{3em}}}$.

$\underset{E}{\underline{\hspace{3em}}}$ + $\underset{F}{\underline{\hspace{3em}}}$ = $\underset{J}{\underline{\hspace{3em}}}$ + $\underset{E_1}{\underline{\hspace{3em}}}$ + $\underset{H}{\underline{\hspace{3em}}}$ = $\underset{J_1}{\underline{\hspace{3em}}}$.

$\underset{E}{\underline{\hspace{3em}}}$ ÷ $\underset{J}{\underline{\hspace{3em}}}$ = $\underset{K}{\underline{\hspace{3em}}}$.

If I = K, then no further calculations on program administration are required.

If I K, then $\underset{I}{\underline{\hspace{3em}}}$ - $\underset{K}{\underline{\hspace{3em}}}$ = $\underset{L}{\underline{\hspace{3em}}}$ x $\underset{F}{\underline{\hspace{3em}}}$ = $\underset{M}{\underline{\hspace{3em}}}$.

If I K, then $\underset{K}{\underline{\hspace{3em}}}$ - $\underset{I}{\underline{\hspace{3em}}}$ = $\underset{N}{\underline{\hspace{3em}}}$ x $\underset{E}{\underline{\hspace{3em}}}$ = $\underset{O}{\underline{\hspace{3em}}}$.

$\underset{E}{\underline{\hspace{3em}}}$ + $\underset{H}{\underline{\hspace{3em}}}$ + $\underset{M}{\underline{\hspace{3em}}}$ - $\underset{O}{\underline{\hspace{3em}}}$ = $\underset{P}{\underline{\hspace{3em}}}$. Item 295 + $\underset{A_3}{\underline{\hspace{3em}}}$ = $\underset{Q}{\underline{\hspace{3em}}}$,

(Items: E + H, Worksheet I-C) x Item 270 = $\underset{T}{\underline{\hspace{3em}}}$ + $\underset{A_2}{\underline{\hspace{3em}}}$ + $\underset{C}{\underline{\hspace{3em}}}$

+ $\underset{P}{\underline{\hspace{3em}}}$ + $\underset{E_1}{\underline{\hspace{3em}}}$ + Item 295 = $\underset{R}{\underline{\hspace{3em}}}$ + $\underset{A_3}{\underline{\hspace{3em}}}$ = $\underset{S}{\underline{\hspace{3em}}}$

+ Item S, Worksheet I-D = $\underset{U}{\underline{\hspace{3em}}}$.

A = Expenditures for teacher salaries

A_1 = Expenditures for substitute salaries for bilingual education

A_2 = Total expenditures for teacher salaries

A_3 = Total operational student FTE in bilingual education

B = Per pupil expenditures for teacher salaries

B_1 = Pupil/Teacher Ratio

C = Expenditures for teacher aide salaries

D = Per pupil expenditures for teacher aide salaries

E = State expenditures specified for program administration

E_1 = Expenditures for general district-wide administration

F = Federal expenditures for program administration

G = Percent state funded FTE teachers of total funded bilingual education teachers

H = Expenditures for coordinators portion of unspecified for bilingual education

I = Percent state funded student FTE of total funded bilingual education student FTE

J = Expenditures for program administration excluding coordinators expenditures

J_1 = Total expenditures for program administration

K = Percent state expenditures for program administration of total administration costs

L = Percent state funded FTE students over percent state program administration expenditure

M = Federal expenditures used to administer state bilingual programs

N = Percent state program administration expenditures over percent state funded FTE students

O = State expenditures used to administer federal bilingual programs

P = Adjusted program administration expenditures

Q = Per pupil expenditures for instructional supplies

R = Total expenditures for bilingual education

S = Per FTE pupil expenditures for bilingual education programs

T = Prorated expenditures for operation and maintenance of plant

U = Program Cost Index

gorical funds for the support of bilingual education. Pertinent data relative to federally-funded student FTE and salaries paid for instruction were also collected from the school districts. Columns 4 and 5 of Section V, Data Collection Instrument No. 2, collected data regarding federally-funded bilingual education programs.

In those cases where New Mexico school districts received both state and federal funds for bilingual education, it became essential to separate the expenditures associated with each funding source. Some districts, because of their lack of funds, had to combine their funding sources to meet their students' needs. For example, the expenditures for administration of both the state- and federally-funded bilingual education programs might have been incurred by only one funding source; yet, the services were rendered to two differently funded bilingual programs.

In Worksheet II, calculations were made to determine if federal expenditures were used to administer state-funded bilingual programs (*Item M*), and if so, were added to the total bilingual education program costs. Calculations were also made to determine if state expenditures were used to administer federally-funded bilingual education programs (*Item D*), and if so, were subtracted from the total bilingual education program costs. These calculations were made to more accurately reflect the actual expenditures associated with state-funded bilingual education programs.

Item U represents the program cost index as opposed to the add-on cost index. The bilingual education program cost index consisted of the total indirect and direct program expenditures per pupil as a ratio to the grades four to six expenditures per pupil.

ANALYSIS

Table 1 (see pages 103-104) presents the bilingual education costs, grades four to six cost per pupil, and bilingual education costs index for New Mexico public school districts.

Column A shows the bilingual education FTE pupils for those districts providing bilingual education programs. Column B shows the state-funded bilingual education program costs. The bilingual education costs per pupil are shown in Column C. The bilingual education add-on or extra costs per pupil are presented in Column D. The regular education program, grades four to six, costs per pupil are shown in Column E. And finally, Column F shows the bilingual education add-on cost index. This figure is determined by dividing the bilingual education add-on cost per pupil (Column D) by the grades four to six cost per pupil (Column E). The bilingual add-on cost index reflects the ratio between the bilingual education add-on costs per pupil and the grades four to six cost per pupil.

Table 1

Bilingual Education Costs, Grades 4-6 Costs Per Pupil And Bilingual Education Cost Index for New Mexico Public School Districts During the 1974-75 School Year

SCHOOL DISTRICT	BILINGUAL EDUCATION A FTE PUPILS	B PROGRAM COSTS	C COST/PUPIL (B÷A)	D ADD-ON COST/PUPIL	GRADES 4-6 E COST/PUPIL	BIL. EDUC. F ADD-ON COST INDEX (D÷E)
Group I 0-200 ADM						
1	3.34	2,929.31	877.04	877.04	1,700.48	.52
2	0	0	0	0	0	0
3	4.79	149.97	31.31	31.31	1,065.25	.03
4	8.34	1,622.55	194.55	193.56	1,554.40	.12
5	3.33	2,222.08	667.29	36.00	1,008.20	.04
6	0	0	0	0	0	0
7	0	0	0	0	0	0
8	0	0	0	0	0	0
9	0	0	0	0	0	0
10	0	0	0	0	0	0
11	7.91	6,599.79	834.36	30.09	1,477.40	.02
12	0	0	0	0	0	0
Group II 201-500 ADM						
13	0	0	0	0	0	0
14	8.00	3,468.80	433.60	433.60	1,042.25	.42
15	19.12	15,352.40	802.95	44.77	794.95	.06
16	0	0	0	0	0	0
17	0	0	0	0	0	0
18	0	0	0	0	0	0
19	0	0	0	0	0	0
20	0	0	0	0	0	0
21	0	0	0	0	0	0
22	0	0	0	0	0	0
23	20.04	12,833.42	640.39	37.43	730.84	.05
24	0	0	0	0	0	0
25	0	0	0	0	0	0
26	1.65	2,706.00	1,640.00	1,640.00	678.13	2.42
27	2.91	3,914.88	1,345.32	1,345.33	1,160.21	1.16
28	0	0	0	0	0	0
29	17.20	6,479.07	376.69	29.59	914.79	.03
30	0	0	0	0	0	0
Group III 501-1000 ADM						
31	5.76	2,490.60	439.26	9.17	705.41	.01
32	17.53	13,996.48	798.43	18.20	887.53	.02
33	24.98	14,779.67	591.66	39.51	729.58	.05
34	15.00	5,751.15	383.41	18.00	872.22	.02
35	8.30	6,272.06	755.67	754.68	771.84	.98
36	42.03	40,412.69	961.52	52.49	1,048.89	.05
37	6.95	5,008.52	720.65	143.67	753.79	.19
38	0	0	0	0	0	0
39	14.33	7,004.36	488.79	16.05	789.80	.02
40	3.50	1,887.20	539.20	539.20	897.61	.60
41	13.80	8,145.73	590.27	117.25	794.70	.15
42	8.58	2,774.26	391.34	391.34	900.87	.43
43	68.28	41,660.36	610.14	10.50	810.33	.01
44	12.53	5,187.29	413.99	148.60	493.84	.30
45	62.84	17,228.21	274.16	71.89	706.01	.10
46	42.87	27,532.40	642.23	32.42	803.79	.04

Table 1 (Continued)

SCHOOL DISTRICT	BILINGUAL EDUCATION A FTE PUPILS	B PROGRAM COSTS	C COST/ PUPIL	D ADD-ON COST/PUPIL	GRADES 4-6 E COST/ PUPIL	BIL. EDUC. F ADD-ON COST INDEX
			(B÷A)			(D÷E)
Group IV 1001-2500 ADM						
47	19.16	10,003.63	522.11	379.05	859.19	.44
48	15.20	3,142.75	206.76	206.76	710.24	.29
49	0	0	0	0	0	0
50	14.7	3,637.37	247.44	0	731.81	0
51	77.95	25,847.44	331.59	131.15	657.04	.20
52	13.50	32,738.58	2,425.08	318.18	756.36	.43
53	5.18	12,503.54	2,413.21	36.61	716.72	.05
54	28.14	14,582.43	518.21	39.98	759.20	.05
55	5.48	4,468.67	815.45	36.13	713.77	.05
56	6.83	757.52	110.91	110.91	653.23	.17
57	0	0	0	0	0	0
58	20.34	17,320.53	851.55	168.03	763.83	.22
59	0	0	0	0	0	0
60	13.16	15,709.49	1,183.73	15.20	684.40	.02
61	0	0	0	0	0	0
Group V 2501-4000 ADM						
62	32.38	28,990.14	895.31	55.28	765.40	.07
63	61.98	28,039.13	452.39	67.77	714.71	.09
64	91.74	151,958.14	1,656.40	315.75	689.53	.45
65	143.92	47,282.04	328.53	65.90	784.03	.08
66	572.44	444,654.21	776.77	235.73	436.88	.54
67	53.92	14,435.46	267.72	24.72	790.25	.03
68	106.38	134,303.69	1,262.49	362.46	670.55	.54
69	37.66	23,735.59	630.26	113.65	789.10	.14
70	0	0	0	0	0	0
71	47.90	6,955.08	145.20	9.87	736.63	.01
72	44.50	35,253.35	792.21	196.40	728.18	.27
73	81.88	56,097.63	685.12	435.68	721.57	.60
Group VI 4001-7500 ADM						
74	0	0	0	0	0	0
75	48.66	58,651.36	1,205.33	352.63	599.92	.59
76	49.82	91,819.75	1,843.03	193.49	708.53	.27
77	114.56	16,982.37	148.24	137.18	874.32	.16
78	245.13	254,479.25	1,038.14	231.75	824.80	.28
79	29.27	8,702.26	297.31	42.02	709.13	.06
80	5.13	3,605.98	702.92	702.92	743.31	.95
81	39.87	35,136.63	881.28	190.09	799.13	.24
Group VII 7501-17500 ADM						
82	14.48	17,710.63	1,223.11	330.87	713.25	.46
83	25.98	26,457.25	1,018.37	19.24	751.46	.02
84	52.27	146,876.61	2,809.96	214.08	718.50	.29
85	176.37	193,303.28	1,096.01	138.01	741.77	.18
86	233.06	94,736.56	406.49	283.51	821.61	.34
87	139.06	64,240.16	461.96	252.55	746.69	.33
Group VIII Over 17500 ADM						
88	455.08	390,859.11	858.88	299.76	761.50	.39
STATEWIDE AVERAGE:	57.53	44,748.18	777.82	205.60	752.93	.27

The direct add-on expenditures for bilingual education included expenditures for teacher aide salaries, specified direct program administration and supplies (see page 107). These expenditures were considered add-on's or extra in providing bilingual education programs. Expenditures for teachers were excluded from these calculations because teachers were considered as part of the regular educational expense which must be incurred whether or not bilingual education programs are provided.

Column A. For the 62 New Mexico public school districts providing bilingual education programs there were 3,566.90 FTE students. There were 26 school districts that were not providing bilingual education programs. Nineteen of the 26 school districts were in Groups I and II, districts with less than 500 ADM students. Bilingual education programs were offered by all but two districts having enrollments greater than 2,500 ADM.

There was an average of 57.53 FTE students in the 62 school districts. The median consisted of 20.19 FTE students. The sizeable difference between the mean (57.53) and the median (20.19) is partially explained by the concentration of bilingual education programs in larger-sized districts.

District 26--a district in Group II--had the fewest FTE students (1.65) enrolled in bilingual education programs. District 66--a district in Group V--had the highest number of FTE students (572.44) enrolled in bilingual programs. The range between the two districts was 570.79 FTE students.

Column C. The highest expenditure for bilingual education was $2,809.96 per pupil in District 84, Group VII. District 3 in Group I was the district with the lowest expenditure at $31.31 per pupil. The mean per pupil expenditure was $777.81. The median per pupil expenditure for bilingual education programs was $658.65. The standard deviation, a measure of variability calculated around the mean, was $559.85.

Column D. The bilingual education add-on cost per pupil differs from the bilingual education cost per pupil in that the add-on costs will always be less because they reflect only a part--the extra costs--in providing a bilingual program over a regular education program. District 5 in Group I provides such an example. The bilingual education costs per pupil for District 5 were $667.29 while the add-on costs were only $36.00 per pupil. In those districts where the bilingual education costs per pupil equaled the add-on costs per pupil, the expenditures for bilingual education were all extra and none of the monies were spent on teachers' salaries.

Column E. For districts offering bilingual programs, District 1 in Group I was the district with the highest expenditure for the regular education program at $1,700.48 per pupil. The mean per pupil expenditure was $752.93. The median per pupil expenditure for grades four to six was \$757.78. The standard deviation was \$212.06.

Column F. The bilingual education add-on cost indices reflect the ratio between the bilingual education add-on cost per pupil and the regular education costs per pupil.

A number of methods exist for computing the state-wide bilingual education add-on cost index. One method is to determine the median add-on cost index, which for this study was 0.18. The two equations below propose alternate methods. The first equation presents the weighted mean program cost index for bilingual education. This equation calculates the mean program cost index at 0.30. The second equation presents the mean add-on cost index for bilingual education. This equation calculated the mean at 0.27. This study utilized this equation to calculate the state-wide add-on cost index because it reflects more accurately the state-wide costs for both the regular education programs, grades four to six, and the add-on costs for bilingual education programs.

$$\text{BCI} = \frac{(\Sigma \text{ Bil. Add-on Costs Per Pupil})}{N} \div \frac{(\Sigma \text{ Grades 4-6 Per Pupil})}{N}$$

BCI = State-wide bilingual education add-on cost index; N = Number of districts providing bilingual education programs.

$$\text{BCI} = \frac{(\Sigma \text{ Bil. Add-on Costs})}{(\Sigma \text{ Bil. Pupil FTE})} \div \frac{(\Sigma \text{ Grades 4-6 Program Cost})}{(\Sigma \text{ Grades 4-6 ADM})}$$

BCI = State-wide bilingual education add-on cost index.

The results of this study indicate that the bilingual education add-on costs per pupil on a state-wide basis are only 27 percent of the regular education program cost per pupil. Or stated differently, it costs \$205.60 per pupil in the form of add-on or extra costs to provide bilingual education programs when compared to the regular education program cost per pupil.

ADD-ON CALCULATION WORKSHEET

Bilingual - Grades 1-3

From Bilingual Worksheet II add Items: _____ C + _____ E + ________ Item 295 = _____ U

÷ _____ A_3 = _____ V ÷ Grades 4-6 Cost/Pupil = _____ W.

_____ R minus _________ U (above) = _____ X + Grades 1-3 Program Cost = _____ Y

÷ Grades 10-12 P/T Ratio = _____ P x Average Teachers Salary = _____ Q

U = Direct add-on expenditures for Bilingual Education
V = Per pupil add-on expenditures for Bilingual Education
W = Add-on cost index for Bilingual Education
X = Non add-on Bilingual Education Expenditures
Y = Adjusted Grades 1-3 Program Cost
Z = Grades 1-3 Cost/Pupil
AA = Cost Index for Grades 1-3

Vocational - Grades 10-12

(Grades 10-12 P/T Ratio - Voc. Ed. P/T Ratio - P/T Ratio Diff.)

÷ Grades 1-12 P/T Ratio = _____ P x Average Teachers Salary = _____ Q

x Number of FTE Vocational Teachers = _____ R.

From Vocational Worksheet IV add Items: _____ 325a + _____ F + _____ H + _____ 321

+ _________ (R above) = _____ S ÷ _____ B_1 = _____ T ÷ Grades 4-6 Cost/Pupil = _____ U.

_____ V minus _________ (S above) = _____ X + Grades 10-12 Program Cost = _____ Y

÷ Grades 10-12 ADM = _____ Z ÷ Grades 4-6 Cost/Pupil = _____ AA.

P = Difference of Grades 10-12 and Vocational Education P/T Ratio as a percent of Grades 10-12 ratio
Q = Teachers' Salary Attributable to Vocational Education Add-on Costs (per teacher)
R = Teacher vocational education add-on costs
S = Direct add-on expenditures for vocational education
T = Per pupil add-on expenditures for vocational education
U = Add-on cost index for vocational education
X = Non add-on vocational education expenditures
Y = Adjusted Grades 10-12 program cost
Z = Grades 10-12 Cost/Pupil
AA = Cost index for Grades 10-12

viewpoint: William Hall

Cross-Cultural Research

A shortcoming in Blanco's paper is perhaps the substantive justification for bicultural-bilingual programs beyond political-social press. The question is, what is the payoff in the cognitive-educational domain for children from such programming? It is on this point that I think Blanco's paper fails to execute its purpose sufficiently.

Is there evidence from the cognitive psychology literature that biculturalism-bilingualism has a positive effect on performance? While emerging, I think there is some data to support an affirmative answer to the question--at least, at the level of examples.

I wish to report in some detail on the research that my colleagues and I completed recently at The Rockefeller University as an example of a piece of research supporting the notion of the effect of an aspect of cultural experience on cognitive performance. The research used a story recall task as the stimulus.

A RESEARCH EXAMPLE

The Story Recall Research

Rationale. A great deal of research in the past decade has been devoted to an evaluation of the significance of dialect for educational performance of Black and White school-children. Two general questions, neither of them definitively resolved, have dominated inquiry in this area. First, what is the linguistic status of "Black English?" Is it a degraded version of standard English or an autonomous linguistic system? Despite a great deal of disagreement about specifics, the bulk of scholarly evidence suggests that Black English is a separate system, historically connected to standard English, but possessing distinct phonological and grammatical forms (Baratz, 1969; Hall and Freedle, 1973; Labov, 1970; see Hall and Turner, 1973, for a dissenting view).

A second question to which psychologists have addressed themselves is: Granted that Black English has at least some distinct features differentiating it from standard English, what are the cognitive and educational implications of agreed upon differences between Black English vernacular and standard English?

Research on the cognitive implications of speaking Black English vernacular has most often concentrated on the role of Black English vernacular and standard English dialects in the comprehension and production of isolated sentences. Although both comprehension and production differences have been reported for some populations and some tasks (Baratz, 1969; Labov, 1972; Osser, Wang and Zaid, 1969), there has been very little evidence to support Baratz's contention that standard test performance of Black English vernacular speakers is systematically depressed by the administration of tests in standard English.

A series of studies conducted by Quay (1971, 1972, 1974) provide negative evidence with respect to the influence of dialect on test performance. Working with lower- and lower-middle-class Black children in Philadelphia, Quay administered the Stanford-Binet test in its standard form or in a Black English vernacular form constructed by W. A. Stewart--a leading spokesman for the view that Black English vernacular constitutes a distinct linguistic system.

In none of her studies did Quay find support for the idea that standardized test instructions depress the performance of her Black subjects, even though a rather extensive range of ages (four to 12) and subject backgrounds were explored. Item analyses were also carried out to see if the more language-dependent items would show a greater dialect effect, but no consistent effects were discernable.

Williams and Rivers* reached exactly the opposite conclusion from a study of dialect variations in the administration of the Boehm Test of Basic Concepts; nonstandard versions of the test produced higher scores than the standard version, so that when presented the test in a nonstandard form (that included vocabulary as well as phonological variations), Williams and Rivers' children scored at levels appropriate to the published norms for children of comparable age and higher socio-economic levels. Since the Stanford-

---

* *The research reported here was supported by grants from the Carnegie Corp. of New York to The Rockefeller University for Michael Cole and William S. Hall and PHS GM 21796 to the laboratories of George A. Miller and Michael Cole at The Rockefeller University.*

Binet and Boehm tests are presumably tapping some of the same cognitive abilities, the results of the Williams and Rivers study are clearly at odds with those produced by Quay.

The present study was designed against this background of incomplete and inconclusive research as a means of extending the lists of tasks for which data on the influence of dialect differences are likely to be influential when the child must retain and then reproduce a substantial body of meaningful material. Hence, a story recall task was selected to study the relations between dialect usage and cognitive performance. As an additional factor, we varied the race of the experimenter to explore the possibility that *who* was speaking might make a difference in the impact of the dialect.

Method

Subjects. The children who participated in the study were selected from two distinct geographical locations within New York City. All of the children were approximately 4 years 6 months of age.

The 16 Black children were residents of a large urban renewal complex in central Harlem attending a federally-sponsored Head Start program for 2½ hours per day. Admission to the program required that the children's parents have incomes within federally set guidelines ($4,000 or less per year for a family of four). Approximately 60 percent of the children were members of families receiving welfare payments. No data were collected on the family incomes of individual children who participated in the study.

The 16 White children were all residents of downtown Manhattan attending a fee-paying, nonprofit co-op nursery housed in the Educational Alliance. Admission to the nursery required the parents of these children to work at a variety of professional and semiprofessional jobs (artists, school teachers, civil servants, etc.). The income of these parents was estimated to be $7,000 per year or above by the program administrator.

Fifty percent of all the subjects were female.

Stimulus Materials. Each child was presented four stories for recall during the course of the experiment. The stories were illustrated using educational materials designed by E. J. Bartlett (1971). As originally designed, the materials constituted a meaningful sequence of pictures with no accompanying text. Special accompanying texts were designed for experimental purposes. Each story contained six picture sequences with an accompanying segment of description and/or dialogue in standard English and Black dialect. In constructing these stories, the grammatical forms described by Baratz (1969), Mitchell (1969) and Hall and Freedle (1973) were used.

Design. Subgroups of four children within each population group were randomly assigned to experimental conditions such that order of exposure to experimenters (Black and White) and dialects (standard English vs. Black English vernacular) were counterbalanced. Imposed on this basic 2 x 2 experimental design was a Latin square assignment of stories to children, such that the four children within each cell of the design received different orders of the presentation of the four stories. This arrangement meant that dialect and race of experimenter were orthogonal variables, but were not orthogonal to the order in which the stories were told and recalled within each subgroup. This limitation of the design was decided upon because our major concern was the influence of dialect and experimenter effects rather than the stories themselves or interactions between the major variables and specific properties of the stories.

Procedure. Each subject participated in two separate sessions, one with a Black and one with a White experimenter. At each session the child was told two of the four stories, one in each of the two dialects. The experimenter escorted the child to a table in an area set off from the classroom, with the explanation that they were going to play some storytelling games.

The subject was shown the picture books and told that he should listen carefully while the story was being told and that then he would have to tell the story back. The instructions were given in the dialect appropriate to the particular experimental condition.

After the child had completed retelling the story, several questions designed to probe recall were presented in the appropriate dialect, regardless of whether or not the information demanded by the question was present in the child's spontaneous recall of the story. All sessions were tape-recorded and transcribed. Questions were asked in the dialect appropriate to the particular experimental condition.

Data Analysis. The data from this experiment were subjected to an analysis of variance employing the independent variables of: (a) racial group membership (Black vs. White), (b) experimenter (Black vs. White) and (c) dialect of stimulus material (standard English vs. Black English vernacular). Performance was not analyzed as a function of stories because the design deliberately confounded the story with the three variables of primary interest.

Results

Spontaneity of Recall. Some of the children were quite hesitant in responding to the experimenter's request for recall. To determine if this hesitancy was related to any of the variables under study, each child's responses to the request for retelling the story were analyzed. A "yes" was assigned to the response if the child had to be prompted, a "no" if the child spontaneously began to retell the story. On the average, 52 percent of the stories were retold spontaneously. There were no statistically reliable variations in spontaneity as a function of any of the independent variables under investigation.

Recall Accuracy. The spontaneous recall of each of the stories was scored for recall accuracy. Each of the phrases used in telling a story was considered an item for recall. The senior author scored each of the 64 response protocols, item by item, to determine a percentage spontaneous recall score for each subject on each story. An item was scored correct if the information contained in the item was also contained in the subject's recall, even if the recall was not verbatim. This scoring scheme was then applied independently by two research assistants who did not know the nature of the study or the hypotheses under consideration. There was a 94 percent overlap between the scores assigned; the senior author's scores (following an arc sine transformation) were then used as the basis for an analysis of variance. The principle results of this analysis in terms of transformed proportions correct are shown in Table 1. The visual impression of an interaction between racial group and dialect obtained from inspection of the table is supported by the analysis of variance which yielded no main effects for racial group or dialect, but a significant Racial Group x Dialect interaction, $F(1, 30)=7.00$, $p<.05$. The Black group performed better in Black English vernacular while the White group performed better in standard English.

Table 1

Mean Scores for Percentage of Correct Information in the Unstructured Recall and Probed Recall Conditions for Two Racial Groups and Two Dialects

Racial group	Black English vernacular	Standard English	M
	Unstructured recall condition		
Black	27.34	21.97	24.66
White	20.09	31.34	25.72
	Probed recall condition		
Black	78.09	59.19	68.64
White	52.44	64.41	58.42

Individual comparisons (Winer, 1971) indicated that: (a) Whites performed better than Blacks in standard English,

F(1, 30)=7.77, p<.05. (b) Blacks performed better than Whites in Black English vernacular, F(1, 30)=6.08, p<.05. (c) Blacks tested in Black English vernacular were equivalent to Whites tested in standard English, F(1, 30)=2.37, p>.10. (d) Whites performed better in standard English than in Black English vernacular, F(1, 30)=16.24, p<.05. When probed with questions there was an overall increase from 25 percent to 63 percent in the proportion of correct information for both racial groups, but all effects of dialect disappeared ($F \leq 1.0$). Nowhere in either dependent variable measuring accuracy of recall did an experimenter effect appear.

Dialect of Output. Each child's language at the time of unstructured recall was classified in one of four categories: standard English, Black English vernacular, mixed dialect and unclassifiable.* Black children spoke predominantly a mixed dialect and Black English vernacular, while White children spoke standard English almost exclusively. Whereas only two of the White children used Black English vernacular forms, all of the Black children did so. However, pure use of Black English vernacular was rare in this sample; all but six of the Black children mixed Black English vernacular and standard forms in the spontaneous recall. As with recall performance, there was no effect of experimenter on language code used. Black children spoke in a mixed dialect 80 percent of the time; White children spoke in standard English 93 percent of the time.

DISCUSSION

It seems reasonable to say that we have shown in this experiment that one's "parent" dialect is the overriding factor in language performance as assessed by this story recall task. Subjects produce utterances primarily in their parent dialect. A caution must be inserted here concerning Black children. These children are bidialectical--their production is a mixture of Black English vernacular and standard English dialects. We do not know the extent to which the same may be said of their parents, but it is certainly true of their community.

The research further demonstrates that when the dialect in which the to-be-remembered story is read does not match the dialect in which the child retells the story, mnemonic interference is produced. The pattern of this interference

---

** Mixed dialect refers to those stories in which subjects used both standard English and Black English vernacular in their spoken recall. Unclassifiable refers to those stories in which subjects' spoken language could not be identified as either standard English, Black English vernacular or mixed dialect.*

as displayed in the table on page 112 clearly supports the "language difference" position discussed in the introduction. The specific pattern of support for this position is worth emphasizing: In line with the language difference hypothesis, White children perform better than Black children only when the two groups are told stories in standard English (see the table). In fact, when stories are presented in Black English vernacular, Black children recall more information than White children. Furthermore, the White children's recall suffers much more from the introduction of Black English vernacular than does the Black children's recall from use of standard English. These recall data are consistent with the language code data in suggesting that while Black children have some knowledge of standard English (they speak a mixed dialect form), the White children are unfamiliar with Black English vernacular. The Black children are, in a sense, bidialectical with Black English vernacular the dominant.

It can be further noted that the code-related mnemonic interference reflected in the table is not a completely general feature of these children's recall. The probed recall data show clearly that the to-be-remembered information has been stored, but was not produced at the time of the initial unstructured recall. When considered together, the pattern of results in the spontaneous and probed recall provides some information as to how the dialect of presentation influences task performance. Our findings, particularly those concerning the bidialecticalism of Black children, are similar to those recently reported by Ciborowski and Choy (1974) for Hawaiian children.

The fact that Blacks recall more information when the task format used is Black English vernacular and that Whites recall more information when the task format used is standard English suggests clear dialect effects. Differences between the dialect of presentation and children's native dialect produce a mnemonic "production deficiency," analogous to the production deficiency for unrelated materials described in the work of Flavell (1970) and Scribner and Cole (1972).

If this argument is correct, it suggests an explanation of the differences between our results and Quay's (1971, 1972, 1974). Because of the nature of IQ tests, they may be a poor arena in which to assess the cognitive consequences of dialect usage.

Other differences between Quay (1971, 1972, 1974) and the present study may also be important. One limitation of the IQ test as an experimental tool is that control over the dialect in which the material is encoded can be manipulated only via the instructions and labeling of individual items: How the child encodes and mentally manipulates these materials is open neither to control nor observation. Moreover, it is not entirely clear that the test used in Quay's work was administered in Black English vernacular. The translations given can perhaps best be described as "mixed" (Quay, 1974). It is also unclear from the directions given in Quay's transcribed version of the Binet test if the complete administration was in Black English vernacular for the dialect condition. For example, were points of clarification during the administration given in the same dialect in which the test was carried out?

Finally, the absence of an effect of the race of the experimenter, accompanied by the strong influence of dialect, adds to the growing literature that questions the general importance of race of experimenter on cognitive performance.

FUTURE RESEARCH

In other articles, it has been indicated that bilingual education can best be saved by longitudinal research, but the kind is not specified. It seems to us that produce-oriented research--longitudinal or otherwise--is not apt to protect bilingual-bicultural education from its enemies. What kind will? A productive future research path might be process-oriented research focused on the components required to do some task and the interaction that accompanies the doing of the task. Research of this variety is currently underway at the following centers (to name a few): (a) The Laboratory of Comparative Human Cognition, The Rockefeller University (Michael Cole, Director); (b) The Laboratory of Human Development and Reading, Harvard University (Courtney Cazden); (c) Department of Sociology, The University of California, San Diego (Aaron Cicourel and Hugh Mehan).

viewpoint: Byron W. Hansford

Meeting the Needs

As Blanco points out, the problems of bilingual education are many and varied. Among those problems are funding (both federal and state), legislation, evaluation, administration and program objectives. I would like to touch upon these topics, but not confine my comments to them exclusively.

Many opponents and proponents of bilingual education have indicated that one major problem of the movement is the terminal nature of federal support for the programs. The history of Title VII legislation does not indicate such an intent. The need for bilingual programs is not uniform throughout this nation and usually where the needs are greater, the local resources are most limited. Blanco has documented this with his data regarding minorities and poverty. There will always be a need for state and local support of these programs, but there will also be a need for federal financial support of them in the foreseeable future. If bilingual education programs were made an integral part of the overall education process--and not just an appendage--they would be much more effective and much less vulnerable to budget cuts.

There is a great scarcity of hard data regarding the effectiveness of bilingual education programs--and undoubtedly this will continue to be a very difficult problem. Since bilingual and other education programs are often restricted by state and federal legislative guidelines, perhaps lawmakers will begin to accept some soft data regarding successes. Highly prescriptive legislation--regardless of what level is involved--cannot mandate successful, high-quality programs. The New York State Education Department's inventory technique is extremely valuable for either providing evidence of the need for bilingual programs or for periodic checks to see that the programs are meeting community needs.

Tests that legislators use for gauging successful programs may be invalid for their purposes. Tests that may be valid for evaluating one school program may be useless for other comparison purposes. Many valid points have been made concerning the cultural bias of many tests. This is further compounded when scores are aggregated on a state or national basis. Lawmakers should be aware than many youngsters reach school-age with little proficiency in *any* language, and determining the dominant language of children is not a simple matter of "testing."

Blanco makes the important point that leadership from the top administration is essential to the success of the program. This is true of any education program, but it is particularly true in bilingual programs which are controversial in many communities. Top administrative leadership cannot only see that the program goes well in school, but they can also engender community support. The bilingual program director should serve as more of a supervisor than an administrator. In that capacity, he can interface with principals, the superintendent and the community. The task of getting community and parental support is particularly important and probably not too difficult since most parents have a concern for their children's education and are anxious to help when asked.

Program design, instructional materials and teacher competencies are other important elements of bilingual education programs. Teaching English as a second language by itself does not constitute a bilingual program, but it may be a first step for many school systems. Although much remains to be done in the area of instructional materials development (including the production of teachers' manuals in the target language), there are now sufficient materials available that the lack of them cannot legitimately be used as an excuse for not having fully bilingual programs. Blanco identified desirable areas of teacher competencies. Although hard to define and measure--I would like to look first for a teacher who will contribute to an improved self-image of the students and then look for other competencies. A policy of the Council of Chief State School Officers on multicultural education states:

> The appreciation of pluralism and a variety of cultural differences does not contradict but supports the value and existence of a united nation committed to the principles of freedom and equality. The Council believes that the development of an understanding and acceptance of cultural, language and life style differences among peoples should be an integral part of the instruction program for every student. Instructional materials which present the positive contributions of all groups living in this country should aim at strengthening the self-identity of each pupil.

The problems of U.S. bilingual education are simple when compared to other countries like Yugoslavia or India. This nation *can* afford to provide an education program designed to meet the needs of each youngster. It cannot afford not to do so.

viewpoint: Protase Woodford

The Importance of Testing

Blanco has described the critical needs of U.S. bilingual education programs. Chief among the needs he listed competent teachers, appropriate didactic materials and procedures and instruments for evaluation. Early in the decade, Andersson and Boyer (1970) insisted that "nothing short of undeniable success will assure bilingual schooling of more than temporary public favor." They set down a list of goals and benefits they felt could reasonably be achieved or demonstrated within six years. Seven years have passed and we have still not been able to offer proof. Least has been done in the areas of evaluation, and few of the evaluation efforts thus far undertaken have rendered encouraging results.

The major evaluation needs of bilingual education include: (a) the determination of children's language dominance; (b) the development of valid measures of language skills in English; (c) the development of skills and subject matter tests appropriate for bilingual children; (d) the assessment of bilingual teachers' language competence; and (e) the design of procedures for assessing individual program effectiveness.

DETERMINATION OF CHILDREN'S LANGUAGE DOMINANCE

One of the first needs of bilingual program directors and others setting up bilingual programs is a method to determine who among the children in the school district is indeed of "limited English speaking ability." This determination needs to be made for a number of reasons. The obvious and most compelling reason is to determine who should go into the program and who should go into the regular mainstream classes. Linked to that basic need is the question of availability of federal and other funds based upon a census identifying children of limited English ability in the school district. Many attempts have been made to develop an instrument that would be both practical and valid for the determination of language dominance. Unfortunately, problems exist with almost all measures thus far developed--particularly in the area of practicality.

In most school districts the determination of language dominance is made on the basis of some kind of interview procedure carried out by bilingual teachers or bilingual teacher aides who, in an unstructured or structured conversation, make a determination of the child's language dominance--a cumbersome, time consuming and unreliable process. It is unreliable because it is difficult for strangers to elicit spoken responses from children and because the scoring is subjective. Since assessing speaking ability is difficult and since there is such a high correlation between listening comprehension ability and speaking ability, a practical procedure for evaluating language dominance might be a reliable measure of listening comprehension. Zirkel (1974) has suggested that a practical approach for determining language dominance would be a test of aural comprehension administered in parallel forms in English and Spanish. The stimulus materials would be utterances in Spanish and English in the alternant forms, but the response choices would be pictures that would accompany the stimulus in each of the languages.

A variety of contexts must be considered in the development of a reliable measure for determining children's language dominance. Such a test must give appropriate weight to the "home" language--the language the child uses in a variety of social settings--and to the "school" language--one with a heavily weighted academic lexicon containing a balance of interrogative, declarative and imperative modes.

DEVELOPMENT OF VALID MEASURES OF LANGUAGE SKILLS IN ENGLISH

A comprehensive battery of skills tests suitable for evaluating bilingual children's abilities in grades one through 12 does not exist--for English, Spanish or any other language. We cannot judge how well bilingual children are performing in a second language unless we know what can be expected of the monolingual native speaker. Base-line data is needed for monolingual native English speakers in the traditional four skills.

Seelye (1977) has emphasized the fact that the states that have mandated bilingual education have by and large mandated "transitional" bilingual education. Regardless of our agreement or disagreement with that concept, children will be moved from a bilingual to a "regular" classroom in most of those states at the end of a specified period of time, or when they have achieved a level of English language skills that will enable them to perform successfully in classes in which instruction is given only in English.

How will it be determined that a child has achieved such a level of English language skills? What are those skills? A major research effort is needed to determine the English language characteristics of the classroom. What must children be able to understand of teacher talk and peer talk in order to function in the classroom? How much English appears in print--either on the blackboard or in texts--that children must be able to read with comprehension? How much actual writing occurs--and how important is child writing to the determination of classroom success?

Though an enormous task, the research effort would be a critical first step in determining what features, skills and what proportions of each would appear in a test of English language skills to be used to determine children's readiness to move into the English-medium classroom. Determination would have to be made of minimal standards. Validation with native English speaking populations would have to be undertaken. Appropriate ethnic and geographic representation would have to be assured in all samplings. Indeed, the task would be a major one, but one that would prove extremely valuable.

The same activity in Spanish would most likely prove much more difficult. The first problem would be to define an appropriate reference group. Although a case may be made for using one or more monolingual Spanish samples from "outside the continental U.S.," there are pressures to limit any comparisons to within county or within state. Lacking a true "monolingual native speaker" reference group, the importance of accurately classifying bilingual children in terms of language dominance becomes even more critical.

DEVELOPMENT OF SKILLS AND SUBJECT MATTER TESTS APPROPRIATE FOR BILINGUAL CHILDREN

Because bilingual children often present different levels of development in two languages across all language skills, the test modality should be such that it will take advantage of all language skills of the examinee. A determination must be made of the optimum modality for assessing skills development and subject matter mastery. For example, a child may understand spoken Portuguese with greater facility than spoken English yet have better developed reading skills in English. A test printed in Portuguese might be less appropriate than one printed in English. Oral Portuguese stimuli with printed English responses might be indicated in such a case.

ASSESSMENT OF BILINGUAL TEACHERS' LANGUAGE COMPETENCE

States mandating bilingual education usually require

teacher competence in two languages. The means whereby that competence is determined varies from state to state. Some states use standardized tests designed for "foreign language" teachers; other states use a face to face interview procedure where the examinee is rated and placed on a proficiency scale such as the one devised by the Foreign Service Institute (FSI).

When an interview procedure is used, great care must be taken in training interviewers and raters and establishing safeguards to assure scoring reliability. Because the interview procedure requires rater judgment, the danger of poor reliability is great. Rigorous training and regular interrater reliability studies must be carried out. Unfortunately, this is not the case in all states where the interview procedure is used.

A rational procedure for determining a minimum level of proficiency is as important as a valid means for assessing language proficiency. In a recent Illinois study, approximately 100 bilingual teachers were given proficiency interviews in English and Spanish. Each interview was rated on the FSI scale by two or more raters. The interviews were recorded and five-minute segments representative of the total interview were drawn. Twenty five-minute segments representing ratings from 1+ to 4+ were assembled in random order with multiple samples in the 2 to 4 range. The 20-interview package was played to a panel of evaluators who were native speakers of the particular language and decision-makers or others with a legitimate interest in bilingual teachers' language proficiency. The panel's task was to rate each interview: "On the basis of the speech sample on the tape would you consider the speaker to have sufficient mastery of the spoken language to function effectively in your program?" With a very small sample of raters for each of the two languages, acceptable ratings clustered in the 2+ to 3+ range. The study did not break down acceptability for programs at different levels--primary, elementary, secondary. However, panels of evaluators, drawn up to represent different levels and different types of programs, could be used in the future to help set minimum levels for their areas of interest.

In the above study, the criterion for both languages was "the educated native speaker" as defined by FSI and Peace Corps. No attempt was made to assess the teacher's ability to understand or speak anything other than "educated native" speech. Indeed there is great controversy over what varieties of the home language (particularly Spanish) the bilingual teacher should have competence in. While there is agreement on the need for the teacher to comprehend the different social and regional varieties of Spanish the child brings to the classroom as well as the child's code switching, there is some disagreement over the version of the home language that the teacher is expected to produce. An effort needs to be made to create listening comprehension exercises that present the varieties--social, regional and age-level--of the language that the teacher will be expected to encounter in the classroom. Such exercises, once developed, can be validated against an outside real-life criterion.

DESIGN PROCEDURES FOR ASSESSING INDIVIDUAL PROGRAM EFFECTIVENESS

Bilingual education programs range from K through grade twelve, from strictly transitional to fully bilingual. The participants in the program range from monolingual English speakers to monolingual speakers of the "home" language. With such an array of goals, curricula and participants, it is clear that no single set of measures can provide appropriate means for assessment. Consideration should be given to the development of item banks, with exercises developed for specific objectives accompanied by interpretive information showing results with populations defined by age and grade level, language dominance and other factors. Item banks of this type would allow each program to assemble measures tailor-made to meet its own assessment needs, to determine how effectively its own objectives are being reached and to identify where there is need for remediation and revision. There are few tests available for use in bilingual programs that meet these criteria and that are valid, reliable and practical.

Compiling hard data of this kind would present evidence that bilingual education does, indeed, work. We can talk about effect, about positive self-image, but at some point we must show that kids who are enrolled in bilingual programs do "better" than their counterparts who have not had that advantage. We must show that they stay in school and that they learn to read and write English, master arithmetic and other subject matter in addition to developing and maintaining skills in their "home" language.

Bibliography

Acts, 63rd Legislature, ch. 392. Austin, TX: Texas State Legislature, 1973.

_____, 64th Legislature, ch. 334. Austin, TX: Texas State Legislature, 1975.

Alaskan Folktales. Austin, TX: DACBE, 1976.

Alatis, J.E. "The Compatibility of TESOL and Bilingual Education." In _English as a Second Language in Bilingual Education_, edited by J.E. Alatis and K. Twadell. Washington, DC: TESOL, 1976.

American Institutes for Research (AIR). _Evaluation of the Impact of ESEA Title VII Spanish/English Bilingual Education Program_. Palo Alto, CA: Author, 1977.

Andersson, T. and M. Boyer. _Bilingual Schooling in the United States, Vol. I_. Austin, TX: Southwest Educational Development Laboratory, 1970.

Bain, B.C. "The Consequence of Unilingualism, Disruptive Bilingualism and Creative Bilingualism for the Development of the Body Schema: A Cross-cultural Study in Canada, Italy and West Germany." Paper presented at the First International Christian University Symposium on Pedolinguistics, Mitaka, Tokyo, Japan, 1976.

_____. "Toward an Integration of Piaget and Vygotsky: Bilingual Considerations." _Linguistics_ 160:5-20, 1975.

Balinsky, W.L. and S.S. Peng. "An Evaluation of Bilingual Education for Spanish-speaking Children." _Urban Education_ 9:3, 271-78, 1974.

Balkan, L. Les effets du bilingüisme français-anglais sur les aptitudes intellectuelles. Brussels: AIMAV, 1970.

Ballesteros, O.A. The Effectiveness of Public School Education for Mexican-American Students as Perceived by Principals of Elementary Schools of Predominantly Mexican-American Enrollment. San Francisco: R & E Research Associates, 1976.

Baratz, J.C. "A Bi-dialectal Task for Determining Language Proficiency in Economically Disadvantaged Negro Children." Child Development 40:889-901, 1969.

Barrera, M. "Bilingual Program Implementation: A Handbook for Teachers and Administrators." Kingsville, TX: Texas A & I University, ms., n.d.

Bartlett, E.J. Adventures in Living: A Preschool Program. New York: Western Publishing Co., 1971.

Ben-Zeev, S. "The Influence of Bilingualism on Cognitive Development and Cognitive Strategy." PhD dissertation [unpublished], University of Chicago, 1972.

_____. "The Effect of Spanish-English Bilingualism in Children from Less Privileged Neighborhoods on Cognitive Development and Cognitive Strategy." Research report to National Institute of Child Health and Human Development, 1975.

_____. "Mechanisms by which Childhood Bilingualism Affects Understanding of Language and Cognitive Structures." Paper presented at SUNY Conference on Bilingualism, Plattsburgh, NY, 1976.

Bernadoni, L.C. The Testing of Bicultural Children. Arlington, VA: ERIC Document Reproduction Service (EDRS), ED 077 977, n.d.

Bernal, E.M., Jr. "Assessing Assessment Instruments: A Chicano Perspective." Paper prepared for the Regional Training Programs to Serve the Bilingual/Bicultural Exceptional Child. Sacramento, CA: Mortel Educational Associates, 1972.

Bilingual Program ARRIBA. Estudio cultural de Puerto Rico. Austin, TX: DACBE, 1973.

The Bilingual Review/La revista bilingüe. Jamaica, NY: Department of Foreign Languages, York College, CUNY.

Bilingual Unit, State Education Department of New York. Puerto Rican History, Civilization and Culture: A Mini-Documentary. Austin, TX: DACBE, 1973.

Blanco, G.M. "Language Proficiency and Linguistics." In Second National Conference of EPDA Bilingual Education Project Directors. Arlington, VA: Center for Applied Linguistics, 1975. [Not for general distribution]

_____. "The Role of Foreign Language Educators in Bilingual Education." In Texas Conference on Coordinating Foreign Languages: A Report of the Proceedings. Austin, TX: Texas Education Agency, 1976.

_____. "The Education Perspective." In Bilingual Education: Current Perspectives, Vol. 4. Arlington, VA: Center for Applied Linguistics, 1977.

Board of Education of the City of Chicago. A Comprehensive Design for Bilingual-Bicultural Education. Chicago: Author, 1974.

Bridging the Asian Language and Cultural Gap: A Handbook for Teachers. Los Angeles: LA Unified School District, 1971-1974.

Brooks, N. Language and Language Learning: Theory and Practice. New York: Harcourt, Brace, and Jovanovich, 1960.

_____. "Parameters of Culture." Based on a talk entitled "Culture vs. Civilization," delivered at the Connecticut Foreign Language Teachers Convention, New Britain, CT, 1972.

Brown, R. "Development of the First Language in the Human Species." American Psychologist 28:2, 97-106, 1973.

CANBBE Northeast Regional Adaptation Center. Carteles puertorriqueños. Austin, TX: DACBE, 1973. [Accompanying Book: Guías para los Carteles puertorriqueños, 1974.]

Cárdenas, B. and J.A. Cárdenas. The Theory of Incompatibilities: A Conceptual Framework for Responding to the Educational Needs of Mexican American Children. San Antonio, TX: Intercultural Development Research Association, n.d.

Carringer, D.C. "Creative Thinking Abilities of Mexican Youth: The Relationship of Bilingualism." Journal of Cross-Cultural Psychology 5:492-504, 1974.

Carroll, J.B. Language and Thought. Englewood Cliffs, NJ: Prentice-Hall, 1965.

Castañeda, A. and others. A New Philosophy of Education. Austin, TX: DACBE, 1975.

Center for Applied Linguistics. Guidelines for the Preparation and Certification of Teachers of Bilingual/Bicultural Education. Arlington, VA: Author, 1974.

_____. A Handbook for Teachers of Vietnamese Students: Hints for Dealing with Cultural Differences in Schools. Arlington, VA: Author, 1975.

_____. "Assessment of Selected Teacher Competencies for Bilingual-Bicultural Education." Final report submitted to the University of Texas at Austin. Arlington, VA: Author, 1976. [For internal use of the University at this time.]

_____. "Response to AIR Study Evaluation of the Impact of ESEA Title VII Spanish/English Bilingual Education Programs." Arlington, VA: Author, 1977 [unpublished memorandum].

Chomsky, N. "Linguistic Theory." In Language Teaching: Broader Contexts. New York: Modern Language Association Materials Center, 1966.

Christian, C.C. "Social and Psychological Implications of Bilingual Literacy." In The Bilingual Child, edited by A. Simões. New York: Academic Press, 1976.

_____ and J.M. Sharp. "Bilingualism in a Pluralistic Society." In Foreign Language Education: A Reappraisal, edited by D.L. Lange. Skokie, IL: National Textbook Co., 1972.

Ciborowski, T. and S. Choy. "Nonstandard English and Free Recall: An Exploratory Study." Journal of Cross-Cultural Psychology 5:271-281, 1974.

Civil Rights Act of 1964. U.S. Congress, P.L. 88-352.

Cohen, A.D. A Sociolinguistic Approach to Bilingual Education. Rowley, MA: Newbury House, 1975.

Colón Sanchez, M. El bilingüismo en Puerto Rico y la actitud de un grupo de jovenes bilingües hacia el idioma vernáculo (Monograph No. 87). Rio Piedros, PR: University of Puerto Rico, 1972.

Committee on Language Attitudes Research Report. Dublin: Irish Government Printing Office, 1975.

Council of Chief State School Officers. Policy Statements. Washington, DC: Author, 1977.

Cruz-Aedo, V. Letter on supply and demand of bilingual education teachers for the state of Texas. Austin, TX: Texas Education Agency, September 10, 1976.

Cummins, J. "The Influence of Bilingualism on Cognitive Growth: A Synthesis of Research Findings and Explanatory Hypothesis." Working Papers on Bilingualism 9:1-43 1976A.

_____. "Sensitivity to Non-verbal Communication as a Factor in Language Learning." Grazer Linguistische Studien No. 3, 1976B.

_____. "Cognitive Factors Associated with the Attainment of Intermediate Levels of Bilingual Skills." Modern Language Journal 61:3-12, 1977A.

_____. "Immersion Education in Ireland: A Critical Review of Macnamara's Findings." Working Papers in Bilingualism 13, 1977B.

_____. "Metalinguistic Development of Children in Bilingual Education Programs: Data from Irish and Canadian (Ukrainian-English) Programs." Paper presented to the Fourth LACUS Forum, Montreal, Canada, 1977C.

_____ and M. Gulutsan. "Some Effects of Bilingualism on Cognitive Functioning." In Bilingualism, Biculturalism and Education, edited by S. Carey. Edmonton, Alberta, Canada: The University of Alberta, 1974.

Cuneo, E. "Bilingual Teaching is a Grave Error." Long Island Press, June 19, 1975, p. 18.

Darcy, N.T. "A Review of the Literature on the Effects of Bilingualism upon the Measurement of Intelligence." Journal of Genetic Psychology 82:21-57, 1953.

De Avila, E.A. and B. Hanassy. Intelligence of Mexican American Children: A Field Study Comparing Neo-Piagetian and Traditional Capacity and Achievement Measures. Austin, TX: DACBE, 1974.

Della-Dora, D. and J.E. House, eds. Education for an Open Society. Washington, DC: Association for Supervision and Curriculum Development, 1974.

Dewey, J. "Aims in Education." In Readings in the Philosophy of Education, edited by J.M. Rich. Belmont, CA: Wadsworth Publishing Co., 1966.

Dickson, D.L. "Methods and Problems of Language Dominance Testing." Materiales en marcha January 1975, pp. 10-16.

Dissemination and Assessment Center for Bilingual Education (DACBE). Directories of Title VII ESEA Bilingual Education Programs: 1969-1976. Austin, TX: Author, 1969-1976.

_____. Evaluation Instruments for Bilingual Education. Austin, TX: Author, 1975.

_____. Publications Catalog. Austin, TX: Author, biennial.

_____. Teacher Education Programs for Bilingual Education in U.S. Colleges and Universities. Austin, TX: Author, 1975, 1976.

Dulay, H. and M.K. Burt. "Errors and Strategies in Child Second Language Acquisition." TESOL Quarterly 8:2, 129-136, 1974.

_____ and others. Why Bilingual Education? A Summary of Research Findings. Berkeley, CA: BABEL/LAU Center, 1976.

Education Service Center, Region II. Adult Education: Bilingual Handbook. Corpus Christi, TX: Author, 1976.

Educational Products Information Exchange Institute. EPIE Form A can be found in Selector's Guide for Educational Materials: Vol. 1, Spanish Language Arts (EPIE Report No. 73). New York: Author, 1976.

_____. Selector's Guide for Bilingual Education Materials, Vol. 2, Spanish "Branch" Programs (EPIE Report No. 74). New York: Author, 1976.

Engle, P.L. The Use of Vernacular Languages in Education: Language Medium in Early School Years for Minority Language Groups (Papers in Applied Linguistics, Bilingual Education Series No. 3). Arlington, VA: Center for Applied Linguistics, 1975.

Ervin-Tripp, S.M. "Structures and Process in Language Acquisition." In Language Acquisition and Communicative Choice, edited by A. Dil. Stanford, CA: Stanford University Press, 1973.

Ethnic Heritage Studies Act. U.S. Congress, P.L. 92-318, 1972.

Feldman, C. and M. Shen. "Some Language-related Cognitive Advantages of Bilingual Five-Year-Olds." Journal of Genetic Psychology 118:234-235, 1971.

Fernández, I. Parental Involvement in Bilingual Education. Arlington, VA: EDRS, ED 088 290, 1973.

Finocchiaro, M. Teaching Children Foreign Languages. New York: McGraw Hill, 1964.

Fishman, J.A. "Bilingual Education: An International Sociological Perspective." Keynote address delivered at the Fifth Annual International Bilingual/Bicultural Education Conference, San Antonio, TX, 1976.

_____. "The Social Science Perspective." In Bilingual Education: Current Perspectives, Vol. 1. Arlington, VA: Center for Applied Linguistics, 1977.

_____ and J. Lovas. "Bilingual Education in Sociolinguistic Perspective." TESOL Quarterly 4:3, 215-222, 1970.

Flavell, J.H. "Developmental Studies in Mediated Memory." In Advances in Child Development and Behavior, Vol. 5, edited by L. Lipsitt and H. Reese. New York: Academic Press, 1970.

Flores Macías, R. "Opinions of Chicano Community Parents on Curriculum and Language Use in Bilingual Preschool Education." Aztlán 4:2, 315-334, 1973.

Foreign Language Annals. New York: American Council on the Teaching of Foreign Languages, six times a year.

Gaarder, A.B. "Linkages between Foreign Language Teaching and Bilingual Education." Bulletin of the Association of Departments of Foreign Languages 6:3, 8-11, 1975.

Gibb, G. "Mathematics and the Bilingual Student." Newsletter of the National Council of Teachers of Mathematics December 1974, pp. 1 and 4.

Gonzales, E. and J. Lezama. The Dual Language Model: A Practical Approach to Bilingual Education. Arlington, VA: EDRS, ED 086 032, 1973.

González, J.M., ed. Reviewing Instructional Materials for Cultural Relevancy. San Antonio, TX: Curriculum Adaptation Network for Bilingual/Bicultural Education, n.d.

———. "Coming of Age in Bilingual/Bicultural Education: A Historical Perspective." Inequality in Education No. 19, February 1975, pp. 5-17.

Greene, J.F. and P.A. Zirkel. Revising the Attitude Toward Bilingual Scale for Use in the Northeast. Arlington, VA: EDRS, ED 076 613, 1973.

Gutiérrez, L. Attitudes Towards Bilingual Education: A Study of Parents with Children in Selected Bilingual Programs. Arlington, VA: EDRS, ED 070 550, 1972.

Hall, V.C. and R.R. Turner. "The Validity of the 'Different Language Explanation' for Poor Scholastic Performance by Black Students." Review of Educational Research 44: 69-81, 1973.

——— and R.O. Freedle. "A Developmental Investigation of Standard and Nonstandard English among Black and White Children." Human Development 16:440-464, 1973.

Halliday, M.A.K. "The Users and Uses of Language." In Readings in the Sociology of Language, edited by J.A. Fishman. The Hague: Mouton, 1968.

Hispania. Worcester, MA: The American Association of Teachers of Spanish and Portuguese, five times a year.

Horn, T.D. "Information Concerning the Language Research Project." Austin, TX: University of Texas at Austin, Learning Disabilities Center, ms., 1976.

Ianco-Worrall, A. "Bilingualism and Cognitive Development." Child Development 43:1390-1400, 1972.

Jaramillo, M-L. "The Future of Bilingual-Bicultural Education." In Ghosts in the Barrio: Issues in Bilingual-Bicultural Education, edited by R. Poblano. San Rafael, CA: Leswing Press, 1973.

Jensen, J.V. "Effects of Childhood Bilingualism." Elementary English 39:132-143, 1962.

Krear, S. and F. Voci. The Role of the Teacher Aide in Second Language Programs. Arlington, VA: EDRS, ED 061 798, 1972.

Labov, W. "The Logic of Non-standard English." In Language and Poverty, edited by F. Williams. Chicago: Markham, 1970.

_____. Language in the Inner City: Studies in the Black English Vernacular. Philadelphia: University of Pennsylvania Press, 1972.

La Fontaine, H. Paraprofessionals: Their Role in ESOL and Bilingual Education. Arlington, VA: EDRS, ED 053 391, 1971.

Lambert, W.E. "Culture and Language as Factors in Learning and Education." In Education of Immigrant Students, edited by A. Wolfgang. Toronto: OISE, 1975.

_____ and G.R. Tucker. Bilingual Education of Children: The St. Lambert Experiment. Rowley, MA: Newbury House, 1972.

Language and Culture: Heritage and Horizons. Middlebury, VT: Northeast Conference on the Teaching of Foreign Languages, 1976.

Liedke, W.W. and L.D. Nelson. "Concept Formation and Bilingualism." Alberta Journal of Educational Research 14: 225-232, 1968.

Litsinger, D.E. The Challenge of Teaching Mexican-American Students. New York: American Book Co., 1973.

Mackey, W.F. Bilingual Education in a Binational School. Rowley, MA: Newbury House, 1972.

Macnamara, J. Bilingualism and Primary Education. Edinburgh, Scotland: Edinburgh University Press, 1966.

_____. "The Bilingual's Linguistic Performance--A Psychological Overview." The Journal of Social Issues 23:2, 121-135, 1967.

Marquevich, P. and S. Spiegel. Multiethnic Studies in the Elementary School Classroom. Pico Rivera, CA: Education in Motion, 1976.

Martin, J.P. A Survey of the Current Study and Teaching of North American Indian Languages in the U.S. and Canada (CAL·ERIC/CLL Series on Languages and Linguistics No. 17). Arlington, VA: Center for Applied Linguistics, 1975.

Matluck, J.H. and B.J. Mace. "Language Characteristics of Mexican-American Children: Implications for Assessment." Journal of School Psychology 11:4, 365-386, 1973.

McBride, Christine. "A Survey of ERIC Reports and Inservice Programs for Teachers in Spanish Bilingual Education Programs." MA report [unpublished], University of Texas at Austin, 1974.

Mitchell, C.I. "Language Behavior in a Black Urban Community." PhD dissertation [unpublished], University of California, Berkeley, 1969.

Milon, J.P. "The Development of Negation in English by a Second Language Learner." TESOL Quarterly 8:2, 137-143, 1974.

Modiano, N. "Reading Comprehension in the National Language: A Comparative Study of Bilingual and All-Spanish Approaches to Reading Instruction in Selected Indian Schools in the Highlands of Chiapas, Mexico." PhD dissertation, New York University, 1966.

Molina, J. Letters of Invitation to Testify before the National Council on Bilingual Education. Washington, DC: U.S. Office of Education, 1976, 1977.

_____. "Proposed Legislative Changes and the Future of Bilingual Education." Address delivered at the Sixth Annual International Bilingual/Bicultural Education Conference, New Orleans, LA, 1977.

Moss, M.H. Tests of Basic Experiences (TOBE). Monterey, CA: CTB/McGraw Hill, Del Norte Research Park, 1970.

Natalicio, D.S. and L.F.S. Natalicio. "A Comparative Study of English Pluralization by Native and Non-native English Speakers." Child Development 42:4, 1302-1306, 1971.

National Council for the Social Studies. Ethnic Studies Curriculum Guidelines: Position Statement. Washington, DC: Author, forthcoming.

National Education Association. The Invisible Minority: Pero no vencibles. Washington, DC: Author, 1966.

_____. "Get Involved in Your Child's School." Hyattsville, MD: Author, American Education Week, n.d.

_____. "Parent-Teacher Relationships." Hyattsville, MD: Author, American Education Week, n.d.

National Institute of Education. Multicultural/Bilingual Division Fiscal Year 1976 Program Plan. Washington, DC: Author, 1976.

Navajo Curriculum Series. Austin, TX: Native American Materials Development Center, DACBE, 1976.

Osser, H. and others. "The Young Child's Ability to Imitate and Comprehend Speech: A Comparison of Two Subcultural Groups." *Child Development* 40:1063-1076, 1969.

Palmer, J.W. *Developing a Competency-Based Bilingual Teacher Training Program*. Arlington, VA: EDRS, ED 108 528, 1975.

Paulston, C.B. *Implications of Language Learning Theory for Language Planning: Concerns in Bilingual Education* (Papers in Applied Linguistics, Bilingual Education Series No. 1). Arlington, VA: Center for Applied Linguistics, 1974.

_____. "Ethnic Relations and Bicultural Education: Accounting for Contradictory Data." In *Proceedings of the First Inter-American Conference on Bilingual Education*, edited by R.C. Troike and N. Modiano. Arlington, VA: Center for Applied Linguistics, 1975.

_____. "Viewpoint: Research." In *Bilingual Education: Current Perspectives, Vol. 2*. Arlington, VA: Center for Applied Linguistics, 1977.

Peal, E. and W.E. Lambert. "The Relation of Bilingualism to Intelligence." *Psychological Monographs* 76:546, 1962.

Peña, A. "Federal Legislative Funding for Bilingual Programs." Paper presented at the International Multilingual-Multicultural Conference in San Diego, CA, 1973.

Pérez, C. "Instructional Methods and Supervised Teaching." In *Second National Conference of EPDA Bilingual Education Project Directors*. Arlington, VA: Center for Applied Linguistics, 1975. [Not for general distribution.]

Perez, C.V. *Auxiliary Personnel in Bilingual Education*. Arlington, VA: EDRS, ED 052 648, 1971.

Pratt, W.T. and J.H. Ramey, eds. *Emerging Role of the Teacher Aide in Navajo Education: A Guide Book*. Arlington, VA: EDRS, ED 099 151, 1974.

Quay, L.C. "Language Dialect, Reinforcement, and the Intelligence Test Performance of Negro Children." *Child Development* 42:5-15, 1971.

_____. "Negro Dialect and Binet Performance in Severely

Disadvantaged Black Four-Year-Olds." Child Development 43:245-250, 1972.

______. "Language Dialect, Age, and Intelligence-Test Performance in Disadvantaged Black Children." Child Development 45:463-468, 1974.

Ramirez, M., III and C. Castañeda. Cultural Democracy, Bicognitive Development, and Education. New York: Academic Press, 1974.

Ramos Perea, I. "El ajuste escolar de los estudiantes migrantes--estudio piloto." Boletín 2:1, 1970.

Reyes, V.H. Bilingual-Bicultural Education: The Chicago Experience. Chicago: Bicultural-Bilingual Studies, 1975.

Rivers, W.M. Teaching Foreign-Language Skills. Chicago: The University of Chicago Press, 1968.

Sánchez, W. "Introducción a las matemáticas modernas para maestros de escuelas primarias." Las Vegas, NM: New Mexico Highlands University, ms., n.d.

San Francisco Unified School District. The Chinese Bilingual Pilot Program, ESEA Title VII, 1974: Program Guide. Arlington, VA: EDRS, ED 098 282, n.d.

Saville, M.R. and R.C. Troike. A Handbook of Bilingual Education. Washington, DC: TESOL, 1971.

Sayler, M.L. Parents: Active Partners in Education. Washington, DC: American Association of Elementary Kindergarten, and Nursery Educators, 1971.

Scott, S. "The Relation of Divergent Thinking to Bilingualism: Cause or Effect?" Research report [unpublished], McGill University, 1973.

Scribner, S. and M. Cole. "Effects of Constrained Recall Training on Children's Performance in a Verbal Memory Task." Child Development 43:845-857, 1972.

Seda Bonilla, E. "Cultural Pluralism and the Education of Puerto Rican Youths." Phi Beta Kappan 53:5, 294-296, 1972.

Seelye, H. Ned. "Viewpoint: Sociology and Education." In Bilingual Education: Current Perspectives, Vol. 1. Arlington, VA: Center for Applied Linguistics, 1977.

Shanker, A. "Bilingual Education: Not 'Why' But 'How'." New York Times, November 3, 1974, section 4, p. 11.

Shuy, R.W. "Problems in Assessing Language Ability in Bilingual Education Programs." Arlington, VA: Center for Applied Linguistics, ms., n.d.

Simons, H.D. "Black Dialect and Reading Interference: A Review and Analysis of the Research Evidence." Ms., 1973.

Skinner, B.F. Verbal Behavior. New York: Appleton-Century-Crofts, 1957.

Skutnabb-Kangas, T. and P. Toukomaa. Teaching Migrant Children's Mother-Tongue and Learning the Language of the Host Country in the Context of the Sociocultural Situation of the Migrant Family. Helsinki: The Finnish National Commission for UNESCO, 1976.

Smith, G.W. and O.L. Caskey. Promising School Practices for Mexican Americans. Austin, TX: Southwest Educational Development Laboratory, 1972.

Spanish Dame Bilingual Bicultural Project. Instructional Guide for the Home Tutor. Austin, TX: DACBE, 1974.

______. Planning the Program with the Home Tutor. Austin, TX: DACBE, 1975.

Spolsky, B. and others. A Model for the Description, Analysis and Perhaps Evaluation of Bilingual Education (Navajo Reading Study Progress Report No. 23). Albuquerque, NM: University of New Mexico, 1974.

State Education Department of New York. Bilingual Education, A Position Paper. Albany, NY: Author, 1972.

Stern, H.H., ed. Foreign Languages in Primary Education: The Teaching of Foreign or Second Languages to Younger Children. Hamburg: UNESCO Institute for Education, 1963.

______. Study E7: Report on Bilingual Education. Quebec: The Quebec Official Publisher, 1973.

Swain, M. "French Immersion Programs Across Canada: Research Findings." Canadian Modern Language Review 31:117-129, 1974.

Systems and Evaluations in Education. New Approaches to Bilingual Bicultural Education. Austin, TX: DACBE, 1974.

Teachers of English to Speakers of Other Languages (TESOL). Position Paper on the Role of English as a Second Language in Bilingual Education. Washington, DC: Author, 1976.

TESOL Quarterly. Washington, DC: TESOL, quarterly.

Texas Education Agency. A Design for Implementing in Public School Curriculum the Concept of Confluence of Texan Cultures. Austin, TX: Author, 1970.

_____. An Orientation to Bilingual Education in Texas: A Training Manual. Austin, TX: Author, 1976.

Thorndike, E.L. and A.I. Gates. "The Ultimate Aims of Education." In Readings in the Philosophy of Education, edited by J.M. Rich. Belmont, CA: Wadsworth Publishing Co., 1966.

Torrance, E.P. and others. "Creative Functioning of Monolingual and Bilingual Children in Singapore." Journal of Educational Psychology 61:72-75, 1970.

Trites, R.L. "Children with Learning Difficulties in Primary French Immersion." Canadian Modern Language Review 33:193-207, 1976.

_____ and M.A. Price. Learning Disabilities Found in Association with French Immersion Programming. Toronto: Ministry of Education, Ontario, 1975.

Troike, R.C. Statement on Linguistic Concerns in Bilingual Education. Arlington, VA: EDRS, ED 093 176, 1974A.

_____. "Research Priorities in Bilingual Education." Arlington, VA: Center for Applied Linguistics, ms., 1974B.

Truong, L. Counseling for Vietnamese Students. Glendale, CA: Glendale Unified School District, n.d.

Tsushima, W.T. and T.P. Hogan. "Verbal Ability and School Achievement of Bilingual and Monolingual Children of Different Ages." Journal of Educational Research 68: 349-353, 1975.

Tucker, G.R. "The Linguistic Perspective." In Bilingual Education: Current Perspectives, Vol. 2. Arlington, VA: Center for Applied Linguistics, 1977.

Tyler, R.W. and other eds. Perspectives of Curriculum Evaluation. Chicago: Rand McNally, 1968.

Ulibarrí, H. Bilingual Education: A Handbook for Education. Arlington, VA: EDRS, ED 038 078, 1970.

UNESCO. The Teaching of Modern Languages (Problems in Education Series Vol. X). Paris: Author, 1955.

U.S. Commission for Civil Rights. A Better Chance to Learn: Bilingual-Bicultural Education (Clearinghouse Publication No. 51). Washington, DC: U.S. Government Printing Office, 1975.

U.S. Department of Health, Education and Welfare. News release announcing interim findings of the AIR Impact Study. Washington, DC, April 18, 1977.

U.S. General Accounting Office (GAO), Comptroller General. Bilingual Education: An Unmet Need. Washington, DC: Author, 1976.

U.S. Office of Education. Programs under Bilingual Education Act: Manual for Project Applicants and Grantees, 1971. Washington, DC: U.S. Government Printing Office, 1971.

______. "Bilingual Education Proposed Regulations." Federal Register 41:69, April 8, 1976.

Valencia, A. Bilingual/Bicultural Education: A Perspective Model in Multicultural America. Arlington, VA: EDRS, ED 028 017, 1969.

______. Bilingual-Bicultural Education for the Spanish-English Bilingual. Las Vegas, NM: New Mexico Highlands University, 1972.

Vázquez, J.A. and L.M. Miller. Letter of invitation sent to directors of ESEA Title VII fellowship programs. Washington, DC: National Institute of Education, 1977.

von Maltitz, F.W. Living and Learning in Two Languages: Bilingual-Bicultural Education in the United States. New York: McGraw Hill, 1975.

Votaw, C.D. "Bibliografía." Washington, DC: Office of the Commonwealth of Puerto Rico, 1976.

Waggoner, D. "Results of the Survey of Languages Supplement to the July 1975 Current Population Survey." Paper presented at the Fifth Annual International Bilingual-Bicultural Conference, San Antonio, TX, 1976. [See also The Linguistic Reporter 19:3, 5, 1976.]

Waserstein, A. "Organizing for Bilingual Education: One Community's Experience." Inequality in Education No. 19, pp. 23-30, February 1975.

Whitman, W. "By Blue Ontario's Shore." Leaves of Grass. New York: Aventin Press, Inc., 1931.

Williams, R. and W. Rivers. "Mismatches in Testing from Black English." Paper presented at the Annual Meeting of the American Psychological Association, Honolulu, HI, 1972.

Winer, B.J. Statistical Principles in Experimental Design. New York: McGraw Hill, 1971.

Zangwill, I. The Melting Pot, Drama in Four Acts. New York: The Macmillan Co., 1909.

Zirkel, P.A. "A Method for Determining and Depicting Language Dominance." TESOL Quarterly 8:1, 7-16, 1974.

Editor's Note: Documents listed with ED numbers are available from EDRS, not published by them.

Acknowledgments

The Center for Applied Linguistics expresses its special appreciation and thanks to those who participated in and prepared papers for the conferences, and to the Steering Committee and Advisors for their valuable suggestions, guidance and moral support throughout the project.

Conference Participants

George Blanco, University of Texas at Austin (Education & Synthesis)

José A. Cárdenas, Intercultural Development Research Association, San Antonio (Education)

James Cummins, University of Alberta (Synthesis)

Charles A. Ferguson, Stanford University (Linguistics)

Lilly Wong Fillmore, University of California, Berkeley (Synthesis)

Joshua A. Fishman, Yeshiva University (Social Sciences)

Joseph O. García, San Diego State University (Education)

Gustavo González, University of California, Santa Barbara (Linguistics)

William Hall, Rockefeller University (Education)

Byron Hansford, Council of Chief State School Officers, D.C. (Education)

Evelyn R. Hatch, University of California, Los Angeles (Linguistics)

Shirley Brice Heath, University of Pennsylvania (Social Sciences & Synthesis)

Editor's Note: The information in parenthesis indicates the particular conference(s) in which individuals were participants.

Richard J. Hiller, Teitelbaum and Hiller, Attorneys at Law, New York City [formerly Puerto Rican Legal Defense and Education Fund] (Law & Synthesis)

Dell Hymes, University of Pennsylvania (Synthesis)

Bea Medicine, University of Wisconsin, Madison (Synthesis)

Hugh Mehan, University of California, San Diego (Social Sciences)

Frederick Mosher, Carnegie Corporation (Synthesis)

Sarah Nieves-Squires, New York University (Social Sciences)

L. Leann Parker, Center for Applied Linguistics (Synthesis)

Christina Bratt Paulston, University of Pittsburgh (Linguistics)

Ernest Pérez, Texas Education Agency, Austin (Synthesis)

Stanley Pottinger, Pottinger and Company [formerly U.S. Department of Justice] (Synthesis)

Roy J. Rodríguez, Office of Civil Rights, DHEW (Law)

Sanford J. Rosen, Rosen, Remcho and Henderson, Attorneys at Law, San Francisco (Law)

Muriel Saville-Troike, Georgetown University (Synthesis)

H. Ned Seelye, Illinois State Department of Bilingual Education, Chicago (Social Sciences)

Roger W. Shuy, Center for Applied Linguistics and Georgetown University (Synthesis)

Edward Steinman, University of Santa Clara School of Law (Law)

Vivien Stewart, Carnegie Corporation (Synthesis)

María Swanson, Bilingual Education Service Center, Arlington Heights, Illinois (Education)

Herbert Teitelbaum, Teitelbaum and Hiller, Attorneys at Law, New York City [formerly Puerto Rican Legal Defense and Education Fund] (Law & Synthesis)

G. Richard Tucker, McGill University, Montreal and Ford Foundation in Cairo (Linguistics)

John Wabaunsee, Native American Rights Fund, Boulder, Colorado (Law)

Brian Weinstein, Howard University (Law)

Protase Woodford, Educational Testing Service, Princeton, New Jersey (Education)

Steering Committee

Mario Anglada, ASPIRA of America, New York City

Will Antell, Minnesota Department of Education, Minneapolis

Joaquín Avila, Mexican American Legal Defense and Education Fund, San Antonio

Arnold Leibowitz, Attorney at Law, D.C.

Roger W. Shuy, Center for Applied Linguistics and Georgetown University

Rudolph C. Troike, Center for Applied Linguistics

L. Leann Parker, Center for Applied Linguistics (Project Coordinator)

Project Advisors

John Lum, San Francisco Unified School District

John Molina, Office of Bilingual Education, USOE

Frederick Mosher, Carnegie Corporation

Sara Sackett, Carnegie Corporation

Vivien Stewart, Carnegie Corporation

Herbert Teitelbaum, Attorney at Law, New York City

Carmen D. Votaw, Office of the Commonwealth of Puerto Rico, D.C.